Q.

WHERE DO THE PAGES OF A BOOK SLEEP?

D1456688

a. under the covers

Published by Bazzill Basics Paper. Featuring artwork by designers Amy Totty, Eva Flake, Kelli Collins, and Pam Black. Photography by Gina Harrop. Layout and design by Shelby Stroud. Product proofing by Jenn Dieu. Edited by Lisa Brennan. A special thanks to Todd Totty, Amy's husband, for letting her be out of sight and out of her mind, "Thanks, Hun!".

Under the Covers

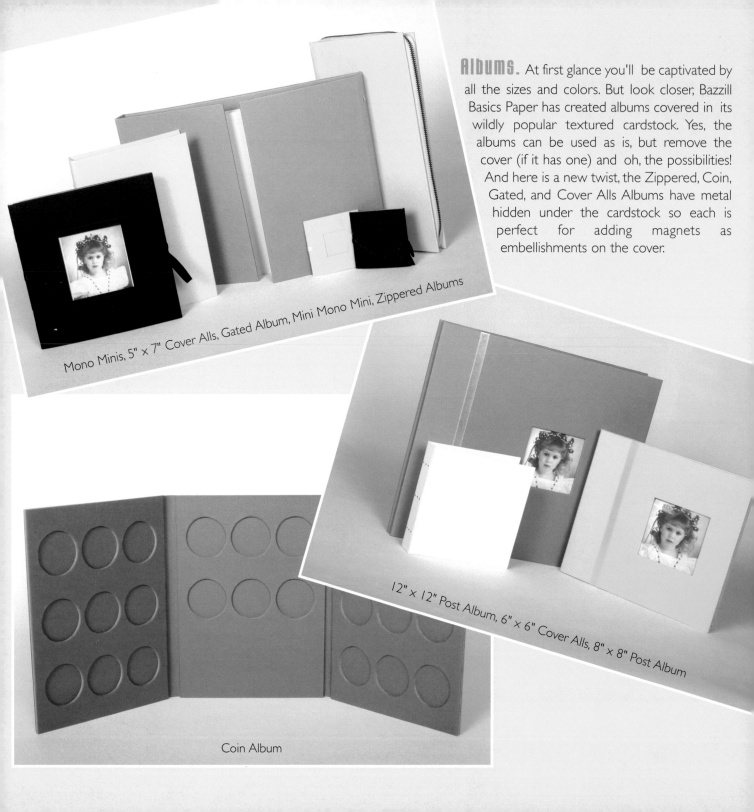

Albums. At first glance you'll be captivated by all the sizes and colors. But look closer, Bazzill Basics Paper has created albums covered in its wildly popular textured cardstock. Yes, the albums can be used as is, but remove the cover (if it has one) and oh, the possibilities! And here is a new twist, the Zippered, Coin, Gated, and Cover Alls Albums have metal hidden under the cardstock so each is perfect for adding magnets as embellishments on the cover.

Mono Minis, 5" x 7" Cover Alls, Gated Album, Mini Mono Mini, Zippered Albums

12" x 12" Post Album, 6" x 6" Cover Alls, 8" x 8" Post Album

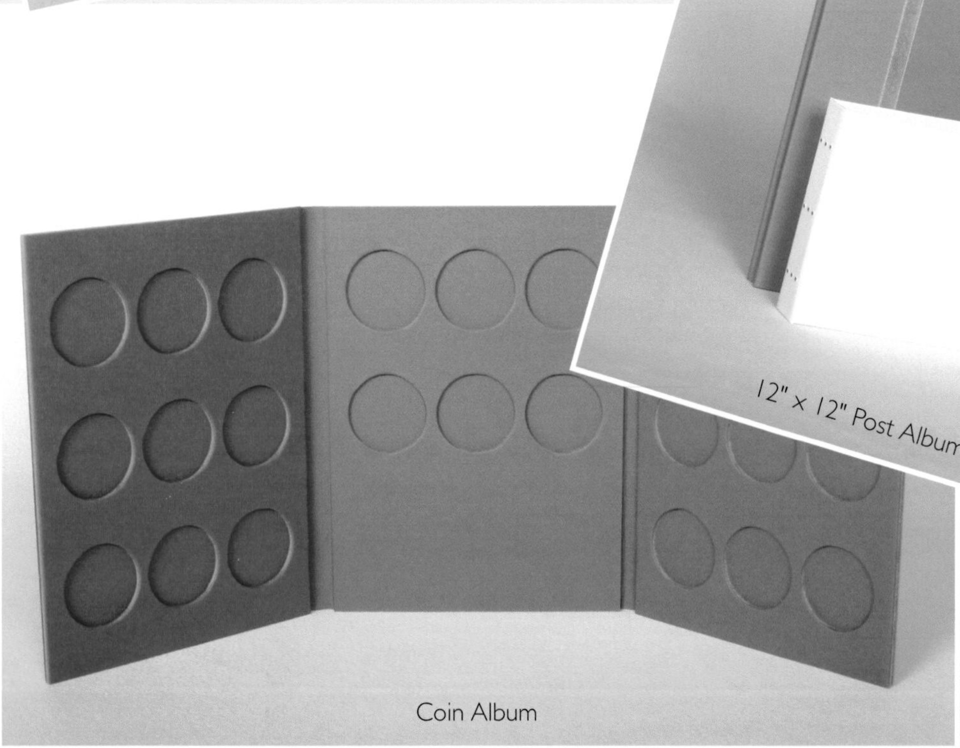

Coin Album

cover to cover

Memories

Artist: Kelli Collins
Bazzill Albums: 6" x 6" Mono Mini, Mini Mono Mini
Album Color: Dark Black
Cardstock Color: Cottonwood
Brads: The Happy Hammer
Label: Dymo
Metal Embellishments and Paint: Making Memories
Rick Rack, Elastic, Ribbons, and Letter "M": Other

PILLOW TALK: Adding a ribbon spine is a fun way to hide the staples holding the book together. Tucking a Mini Mono Mini inside the window of the larger album is also fun. This creates a hidden space to add personal journaling or additional photos.

Pillow Talk: It's sad to admit but aside from weddings and graduations, thank you cards are rarely given anymore. As a little girl, my mother taught me the importance of sending thank you notes, not only for gifts, but for the reward of good friendship. Even to this day, I love the fact that such a simple gesture can brighten someone's day.

Thank You

Artist: Amy Totty
Bazzill Album: Mini Mono Mini
Album Color: Dark Black, Parakeet
Cardstock Colors: White/KI
Jellys: Making Memories
Ribbon: Offray

2 Special

Artist: Amy Totty
Bazzill Album: 6" x 6" Mono Mini
Album Color: Parakeet
Flower: Other
Brad: All My Memories
Mailbox Letters, Metal Word: Making Memories
Ribbon: May Arts

Pillow Talk: I cannot stop making books about my niece!! It is becoming addictive. Those marshmallow cheeks and big blue eyes; she takes the most expressive photographs. It's almost as if those eyes hold the answers to every question I could ever ask. I cannot wait to see what a wonderful young lady she becomes.

Pillow Talk: My husband sings goofy songs almost every day. He sings to wake up the kids. He sings to play with them and he sings to cheer them up. He loves to cook and the songs that come from the kitchen are our favorites! We have already forgotten a lot of his songs so I thought we needed to start recording the words to those silly ditties. One day we will look back and laugh probably harder than we do now.

Silly Songs by Dad

Artist: Amy Totty
Bazzill Album: 8" x 8" Mega Mono Mini
Album Color: Parakeet
Pattern Paper: American Craft
Sticker: Doodlebug Design Inc
Bazzill Chips: Bazzill

Beach Buddies

Artist: Pam Black
Bazzill Album: 8" x 8" Mono Mini
Album Color: Dark Tangerine
Cardstock Colors: Dark Tangerine, Jacaranda
Printed Paper: Paper Fever
Rubber Stamps: Stampotique Originals, Stamper's Anonymous
Ink: Tsukineko, Ranger
Fonts: 2Peas - Red Dog, AL Worn Machine
Silk Flower, Silver Eyelets, Rub-Ons: Making Memories
Waxy Flax: Scrapworks
Mini Brads: American Tag
Ultra Thick Embossing Powder: Suze Weinberg
Buttons, Word Pebble: Junkitz
Staples: Office Supply Store
Ribbons: May Arts, Raffitt Ribbons, Other

Pillow Talk: Try mounting paper on a cardboard coaster, then round the corners of the paper to match the coaster. Sand and ink the edges using Van Dyke Brown to color in the white edges. Use several coats of ultra thick embossing powder to make the tile look like beach glass. Immediately after heating the final coat of embossing powder, press a textured rubber stamp (use embossing ink on the stamp so it will release) into some of the edges to make it look like it has cracked.

Pillow Talk: In order to achieve a white-washed look, lightly dry brush white acrylic paint over the book and metal frame. Sand the metal frame and the "metal F" to remove some of the finish so that a little bit of metal peeks through.

Friend

Artist: Eva Flake
Bazzill Album: 6" x 6" Mono Mini
Album Color: Dark Tangerine
Cardstock Colors: Parakeet, Travertine
Printed Paper: Chatterbox
Rubber Stamps: Hero Arts
Ink: Tsukineko
Metal Frame: Making Memories
Ribbon Corners: Making Memories
Bazzill Chips: Bazzill
Metal Letter: Colorbök
Acrylic Paint: Delta
Foam Flower Stamp: Unknown
Ribbon: May Arts
Fiber: Fiber Scraps

I Adore You

Artist: Pam Black
Bazzill Album: 8" x 8" Mono Mini
Album Color: Jacaranda
Cardstock Color: Jacaranda
Printed Papers: SEI
Ink: ColorBox
Rub-Ons: Making Memories
Metal Washer, Sticker: Making Memories
Mini-Brads: American Tag
Button: SEI
Ribbons: May Arts
Silk Flowers: Other

Pillow Talk: To add highlight and texture to the cardstock, use the direct-to-paper method of swiping a chalk based ink pad (instead of paint) across the front of the book and along the edges.

Pillow Talk: Every Mom has hopes and dreams for her baby's future. I wanted to write down my feelings for each of my children in their own book. I have lots of advice, and even more expressions of love than these books can hold -- but it's a start. I try and write something down whenever I think of it so that I don't forget the little details. The fact that these handy albums are small is even better.

Where These Toes Will Take You

Artist: Amy Totty

#1 Bazzill Album: 5" x 7" Mono Mini
Album Color: Typhoon
Jump Ring: Junkitz
Ribbon: May Arts

#2 Bazzill Album: 5" x 7" Mono Mini
Album Color: Dark Black
Jump Ring: Junkitz
Ribbon: May Arts

#3 Bazzill Album: 5" x 7" Mono Mini
Album Color: Dark Sand
Jump Ring: Junkitz
Ribbon: May Arts

#4 Bazzill Album: 6" x 6" Mono Mini
Album Color: Romance
Jump Ring: Junkitz
Ribbon: May Arts

Many Faces Of Kooper Totty

Artist: Amy Totty
Bazzill Album: 8" x 8" Mega Mono Mini
Album Color: Typhoon
Cardstock Colors: Dark Sand, Light Spruce, Light Denim, Dark Spruce, Dark Chocolate
Pattern Paper: Chatterbox
Stamps: Hero Arts
Ink: Ranger
Brads: All My Memories
Wide Twill: Other

Pillow Talk: My youngest son, Kooper, has the uncanny ability to make the cutest faces anytime he is put on the spot. Of all the faces he makes, the one that is my favorite is the 'I just got caught' look. He will put his index fingers to his cheeks and give this smile that makes it impossible for me to get after him. Heaven help me if he still possesses this charming little gift when he turns 16!

Pillow Talk: This book is the perfect way to treasure all of the memories surrounding the Thanksgiving holidays. To create an album with a feeling of fall chose colors reminiscent of the season. Rake a brown ink pad along the edges of the book and accent pieces for a distressed, old-time feel.

Thanksgiving Memories

Artist: Eva Flake
Bazzill Album: 6"x 6" Mono Mini
Album Color: Dark Olive
Cardstock Colors: Brick Road, Rusted
Printed Paper: Rusty Pickle
Stamps: Hero Arts
Ink: Ranger, Tsukineko
Labels: Dymo
Square Brads: All My Memories
Definition: Foofala
Fabric, Round Metal Tiles, Accent Card: Other

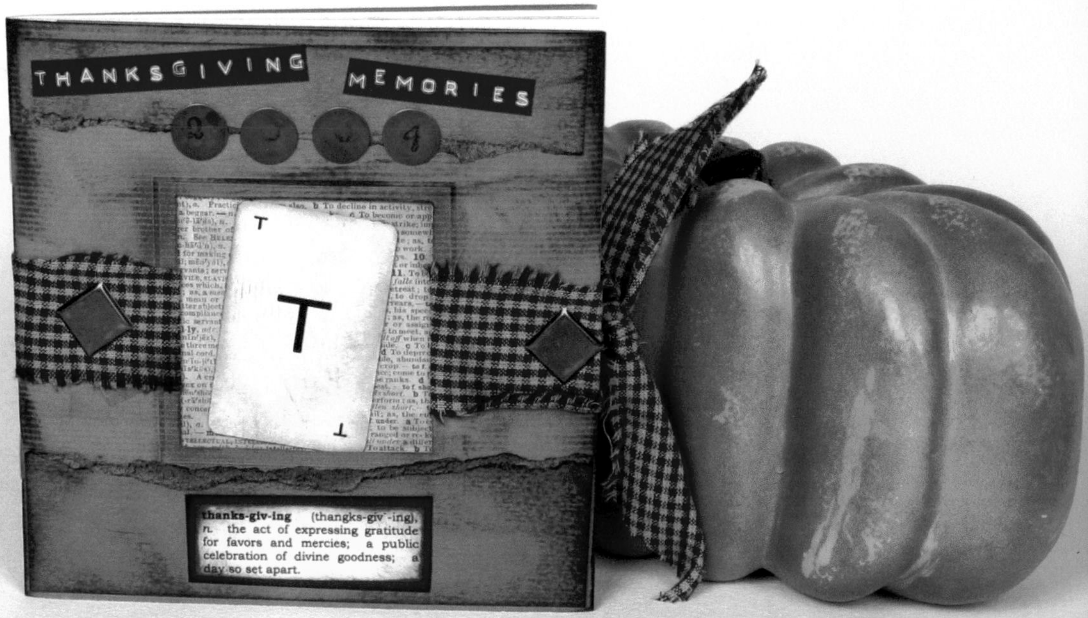

Jenaye

Artist: Kelli Collins
Bazzill Album: 8" x 8" Mono Mini
Album Color: Dark Chocolate
Bazzill Cardstock Color: Green Tea
Bazzill Chips: Bazzill
Buttons: Bazzill
Brads: The Happy Hammer
Printed Paper: SEI
Stamps: Post Modern Design
Ink: Stewart Superior
Metal Clips: 7 gypsies
Ribbon, Trim, Rick Rack, Elastic, Pink
Ticket: Other

Pillow Talk: Bazzill Chips covered with printed paper or cardstock make a great dimensional embellishment. Attach the paper to the chip using Diamond Glaze or a tacky tape for a secure bond.

FULL
coverage

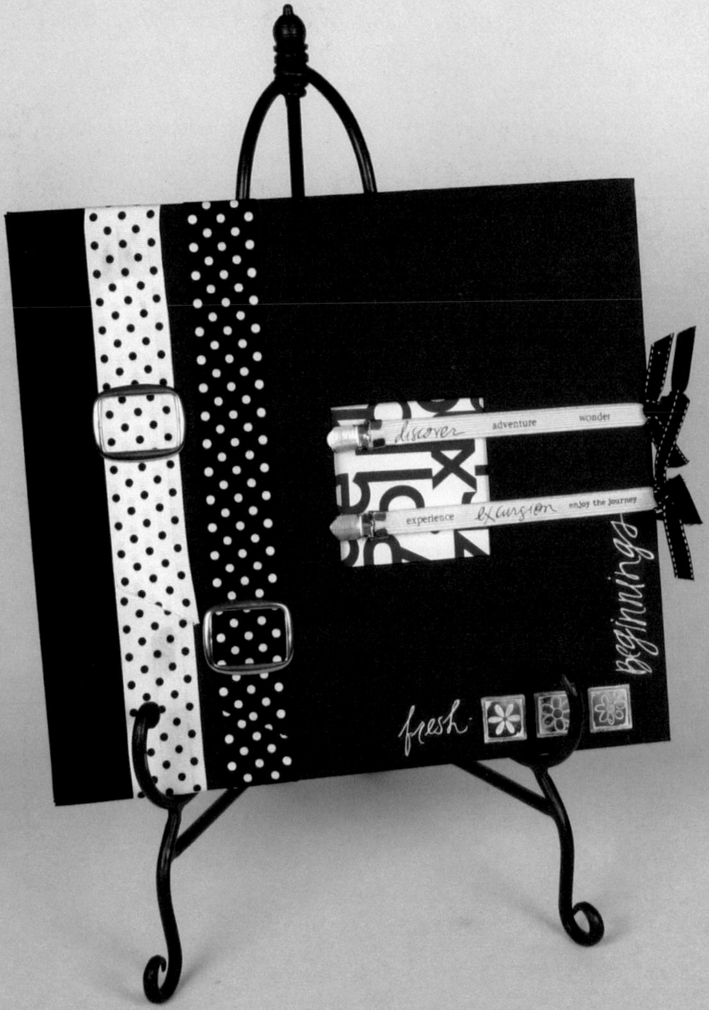

Fresh Beginnings

Artist: Amy Totty
Bazzill Album: 12" x 12" Post
Album Color: Raven
Printed Paper: KI Memories
Paint: Delta
Rub-Ons, Mini Plaques: Making Memories
Elastic, Buckles: Other
Ribbon: May Arts, Mokuba, Other

Pillow Talk: I have a friend, who has a daughter that just graduated from college and landed herself an amazing job on the east coast. I made this going away gift to celebrate the next exciting chapter in her life. I included some family photos in the first few pages, great quotes about careers, success, and the strengths of being independent in the middle, and I left room at the end to add more once she gets started in her new job and begins exploring her new city. Oh, to be young again!

Pillow Talk: I tucked a little welcome note into the pink envelope on the front of this book for my newest granddaughter. Her nursery was designed using these sweet colors and I added tons of ribbon! Try using an album like this in a non-traditional way. It looks perfect on her nightstand, and I hope she will cherish my first sentiments years from now. I love you, Hadley!

Baby H

Artist: Pam Black
Bazzill Album: 8" x 8" Post
Album Color: Raven
Cardstock Color: Raven
Envelope: Waste Not Paper
Printed Papers: Deluxe Designs, Anna Griffin
Transparency: Creative Imagination
Ink: Ranger
Ticket Stubs: Other
Bazzill Chips: Bazzill
Flowers, Metal Letter: Making Memories
Mini Brad: American Tag
Diamond Glaze: Judi Kins
Staples: Office Supply Store
Large Black Snap: Fabric Store
Ribbons: May Arts, Mokuba, Other

Lauren

Artist: Amy Totty
Bazzill Album: 12" x 12" Post
Album Color: Romance
Bazzill Chips: Bazzill
Ink: Ranger
Flowers: Other
Beads: All My Memories
Stamp: Hot Potatoes
Stickers: Making Memories
Charms: Pressed Petals
Ribbon: May Arts

Pillow Talk: On my husband's side of the family, his grandparents had 27 grandchildren. Of all 27 grandchildren, only three were girls. I knew this before we were married but still had high hopes that we would one day be blessed with one of the rare commodities that seems to elude his family. Well, truth be told, I informed my husband we were just going to keep having kids until we had a girl. The fourth time was a charm -- and we got her. She is the perfect balance of just enough rough and tumble to keep up with four brothers and pink dress wearing girlie girl. This book celebrates my little girl, and for me, celebrates the fact that I don't have to spend the rest of my life living in a house full of boys. Girl Power!

Pillow Talk: I thought it would be fun to not only celebrate Konner's 10th birthday, but to also celebrate his new double digit age. Sometimes the smallest, most unusual things in life can be the cutest ones to point out as themes in your books.

Konner

Artist: Amy Totty
Bazzill Album: 8" x 8" Post
Album Color: Typhoon
Paint: Delta
Friction Tape: Other
Ribbon, Book Tape, Rub-Ons, Mailbox
Letters: Making Memories

Mason I. Davis

Artist: Eva Flake
Bazzill Album: 8" x 8" Post
Album Color: Raven
Cardstock Colors: Travertine
Stamps: Hero Arts, Postmodern Design
Ink: Ranger
Name Plate: Li'l Davis Designs
Brads: The Happy Hammer
Acrylic Paint: Delta
Buckle, Twill Tape: Other

Pillow Talk: I envisioned decorating this album so that it would project a strong, classic, masculine feeling. I really had to restrain myself to keep from adding too many embellishments (which is a tendency of mine!). I created this album for my father and I plan to fill it with many photos of his childhood.

Pillow Talk: In my honest opinion, there is no better season than fall. Even living in the desert, I still feel there is electricity in the air when fall arrives. I love it all: hearing football on TV, unpacking sweaters, knowing the kids are back in school, enjoying shorter days, and cooking stew in the crock pot on Sundays. To me, these are all things that are signs that life is slowing down and it is time to begin taking the opportunity to savor all the bounties in which we have been blessed.

Season of Change

Artist: Amy Totty
Bazzill Album: 8" x 8" Post
Album Color: Hillary
Flowers, Rick Rack: Other
Ribbon: Other
Rub-Ons: Making Memories

At the Beach

Artist: Pam Black
Bazzill Album: 8"x 8" Post
Album Color: Pomegranate
Cardstock Color: Maraschino
Printed Paper: Mara-Mi
Stamps: Hot Potatoes
Paint: Making Memories
Metal Molding, Acrylic Paint, Button: Making Memories
Charm: Blue Moon Beads
Buckle: KI Memories
Word Pebble: Li'l Davis Designs
Rub-Ons: Autumn Leaves
Silk Flower and Ribbon: Others
Ribbons: May Arts
Rick Rack: Other

Pillow Talk: I just love these colors together, it makes my heart sing! I wanted to use the girls' picture from the beach because I thought it was a perfect accent for the cute little red album. Then I found this incredible new ribbon from May Arts. Sometimes it's just easier to work with tried and true color combinations.

Pillow Talk: Using a Japanese screw punch, create two holes on both sides of the ribbon and tie pieces of ribbon or fiber through the cover, knotting it on the front side of the album. This is a great place to hang little do-dads and other personal memorabilia.

Girlfriends

Artist: Kelli Collins
Bazzill Album: 12" x 12" Post
Album Color: Pomegranate
Stamps: Plaid, Hampton Arts, Unknown
Ink: Ranger
Label: Dymo
Letter Tile: Paper Bliss
Letter Labels: me & my big ideas
Letter Bead: Bits & Pieces
Jump Ring: Junkitz
Round Disc: Rollabind
Label Plate, Safety Pin: Li'l Davis Designs
Small Metal Rim Tag: EK Success
Flower Brads, Flower Button, Rub-On Letters, Metal Hinges, Metal Photo Corners: Making Memories
Letter Card, Ribbon, Elastic, Silver Safety Pin, Rick Rack: Other
Diamond Glaze: Judikins

Me

Artist: Amy Totty
Bazzill Album: 8" x 8" Post
Album Color: Bazzill White
Cardstock Colors: Hazard, White/Kl, Green Tea/Kl
Paint: Delta
Metal Words: Pressed Petals
Stencil: Making Memories
Twill, Safety Pins, Charms: Other
Metal Paper: Making Memories
Ribbon: May Arts, Offray, Other

Pillow Talk: This album is super-fast to decorate. The album is already covered in Bazzill Basics cardstock so anything you can do to a layout, you can do to a Bazzill album! I painted on this one and wrapped ribbon around to the front and tied bows. Since orange is my F-A-V-O-R-I-T-E color and the album is about me, why not use what I love? Each Bazzill album is so much fun to transform into a style that just screams "YOU".

Pillow Talk: Create three holes in the spine of the album using a piercing tool. Sew through the holes using the butterfly stitch to attach the elastic and Bazzill Boshers to the album.

Art Album

Artist: Kelli Collins
Bazzill Album: 8" x 8" Post
Binding: Butterfly Stitch
Album Color: Baby Blue
Boshers: Bazzill
Printed Paper: BASICGREY
Sticker: Creative Imaginations
Letter Tiles: Westrim Craft
Clip Board, Elastic: Other

PHOTOGRAPHY is my canvas and YOU my Art.
Abercrombie
ART
baldessamat-RF

12 Days of Christmas

Artist: Amy Totty
Bazzill Album: 12" x 12" Post
Album Color: Pomegranate
Cardstock Colors: Dark Black, Julep
Mailbox Letters: Making Memories
Stencil: Making Memories
Tree Charms: Making Memories
Buttons, Wide Bias Tape, Fabric,
Printed Twill: Other
Letter Tiles: Other

Pillow Talk: I have a collection of stories that I have saved over the years that I love to tell during this wonderful time of year. I pick one story to tell each evening during the 12 days of Christmas and read it to my kids. As a gift, I made this album for my sister now that she has a family of her own. I have included all of our family's favorite stories and traditions, and hope she will add even more of her own favorites.

cover + pages

BOOK

Good Luck

Artist: Amy Totty
Bazzill album: 5" x 7" Cover Alls
Album Color: Raven
Binding: Ribbon Over Spine
Printed Paper: Mara-Mi
Safety Pins and Tags: Making Memories
Small Twill: Other
Large and Small Rick Rack, Elastic: Other
Ribbon: May Arts, Midori

Pillow Talk: I thought it would be fun to make a book for a friend of mine who is getting married. I used her favorite colors, which really match her fun and outgoing personality. It wouldn't surprise me if these colors end up being her wedding colors. I am going to fill this book with marriage advice from all her married friends. Good Luck, Heidi!

Pillow Talk: I love the binding of this book. It is a little harder to do but it has such a fun look. You can use 2, 3, 4, even 5 pieces of ribbon or twill in a variety of widths. The versatility of this binding is what is so fresh and new. The possibilities are endless!

Friends

Artist: Amy Totty
Bazzill Album: 6" x 6" Cover Alls
Album Color: Raven
Binding: Hop, Skip, & A Jump
Paint: Delta
Foam Stamp, Magnets: Other
Black Safety Pins, Elastic,
Twill Tape: Other
Small Safety Pins: Dritz
Alphabet: Junkitz

Princess Lauren

Artist: Amy Totty
Bazzill Album: 6" x 6" Cover Alls
Album Color: Baby Pink
Binding: Ribbon Over Spine
Printed Paper: K & Company
Ink: Tsukineko
Metal Word, Metal Letter: Pressed Petals
Rick Rack: Other
Ribbon: May Arts, Offray

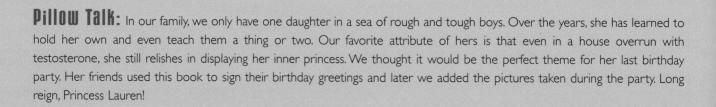

Pillow Talk: In our family, we only have one daughter in a sea of rough and tough boys. Over the years, she has learned to hold her own and even teach them a thing or two. Our favorite attribute of hers is that even in a house overrun with testosterone, she still relishes in displaying her inner princess. We thought it would be the perfect theme for her last birthday party. Her friends used this book to sign their birthday greetings and later we added the pictures taken during the party. Long reign, Princess Lauren!

Pillow Talk: Each Cover Alls Album is lined with metal, making it the perfect place to display magnets. I decorated this album for my daughter by adding a magnet to the pencil so she can store it on the front when she is done using it. I also added a magnet clip so she can clip important items to the front for easy reference. Would you have guessed the silk flower is a magnet, too? What a fun, unique way to decorate the cover of a journal!

Emmalee's Journal

Artist: Eva Flake
Bazzill Album: 5" x 7" Cover Alls
Album Color: Romance
Binding: Fast Binding
Cardstock Colors: Romance
Printed Papers: Making Memories
Rubber Stamps: Hero Arts
Ink: Ranger
Rub-Ons: Making Memories
Name Plate: Li'l Davis Designs
Brad: All My Memories
Ribbon: May Arts, Midori
Magnet Clip, Silk Flower, Pencil, Rick Rack, Accent Card: Other

Grandma's Cookin'

Artist: Amy Totty
Bazzill Album: 6" x 6" Cover Alls
Album Color: Walnut
Binding: Butterfly
Printed Paper: K and Company
Ink: Ranger
Waxed Linen: Other
Stickers: K and Company
Tabs: 7 gypsies
Ribbon: May Arts

Pillow Talk: So many of my memories are centered around the kitchen. Family gatherings at Grandma's house were never complete without her famous potato salad, or the incredible aroma of her homemade rolls. Creating a cookbook using this album is a great gift idea for a newlywed couple, or as a house warming gift. Everyone can use a tried and trusted recipe!

Pillow Talk: My travel journal documents all of the fun I have had traveling through the years. The colors for the cover were chosen from the photo of the old window in the brick building. By selecting really fun colors of ribbon and twill to bind the book, I was able to match the color scheme of the cover. In order to continue the charm reflected in the photo, the cover was distressed by sanding the printed paper and photo. Black and brown ink pads were raked along the edges to add even more of an aged look.

Travel Journal

Artist: Eva Flake
Bazzill Album: 5" x 7" Cover Alls
Album Color: Raven
Binding: Fast Binding
Cardstock Colors: Brick Road
Printed Paper: Rusty Pickle, Deluxe Designs
Ink: Ranger
Metal Plaque: Making Memories
Rub-Ons: Making Memories
Frames: Li'l Davis Designs
Labels: Dymo
Ribbon: May Arts
Twill: Other

100% Boy

Artist: Amy Totty
Bazzill Album: 6" x 6" Cover Alls
Album Color: Jacaranda
Binding: Butterfly and Reverse Butterfly Stitch
Cardstock Colors: Starmist, Parakeet, Hillary
Printed Paper: Daisy D's
Frame: Pebbles, Inc.
Letters: Making Memories
Diamond Glaze: Judi Kins
Stickers: Bo Bunny
Twill: Other

Pillow Talk: With a house full of boys we have seen everything from trying to jump off the roof to having to remove a pinto bean from a nose. Even with so many displays of unbridled testosterone, there is a sweet, almost cherub-like quality that each of our boys possess. It always makes me smile inside when I see it. Small things, like an "I love you, Mom" for no reason, are my favorite. I am proud to say that each of my sons still give their Mom a hug before leaving the house -- even in front of their friends. It is because of moments like these that I beam on the inside knowing the kind of sensitive and loving husbands and fathers they will become.

Pillow Talk: In August of 2003, our family went on our first "real" family vacation to San Diego. We made every part of it an adventure, right down to the drive there. Family vacations can provide such incredible memories, so why wouldn't you want to jot down as many stories as possible? We took so many pictures on this trip I can create "San Diego 2003" Volumes 2 and 3!

San Diego 2003

Artist: Amy Totty
Bazzill Album: 6" x 6" Cover Alls
Album Color: Walnut
Binding: Ribbon Over Spine
Stamps: Technique Tuesday
Ink: Ranger
Metal Bar: 7 gypsies
Printed Paper, Tags, Stickers: SEI
Small Rick Rack, Small Twill: Other

Holiday Traditions

Artist: Amy Totty
Bazzill Album: 6" x 6" Cover Alls
Album Color: Ivy
Binding: Butterfly Stitch
Pattern Paper: The Scrapbook Wizard
Greenery, Waxed Linen: Other
Wide Twill: Technique Tuesday
Rub-Ons: Autumn Leaves

Pillow Talk: In our home, Christmas is everyone's favorite holiday. Every Christmas has its own spirit about it and we always make sure to record each one. Every Christmas Eve, after going out for our traditional Christmas lights trip in our pajamas, we sit around the fire and start talking about all things we are looking forward to the next morning.

Pillow Talk: I grew up hearing so many great stories about my grandparents. These stories always fascinated me because they seemed so surreal, yet I know one day when I tell my grandkids stories they will have similar feelings. I don't want to lose the great stories of my grandparents. Writing down my history is becoming even more important to me as I get older.

Bills' Family Heritage

Artist: Amy Totty
Bazzill Album: 5" x 7" Cover Alls
Album Color: Walnut
Binding: Reverse Butterfly Stitch
Printed Paper: Chatterbox
Ink: Tsukineko, Ranger
Charms: All My Memories
Rusty Keys: Rusty Pickle
Stamps: Technique Tuesday
Hook Tape: Other
Image Transfer Pen: Eberhard Faber Inc.
Ribbon: May Arts

The 5 Ws

Artist: Amy Totty
Bazzill Album: 6" x 6" Cover Alls
Album Color: Pomegranate
Binding: Ribbon Over Spine
Cardstock: Java, Baby Pink
Pattern Paper: Cross My Heart
Charms: All My Memories
Bazzill Chips: Bazzill
Twill: Other
Ribbon: May Arts, Offray

Pillow Talk: I have a little secret…my scrapbook room is a little unorganized. Whenever a creative mood strikes, I run into my room and paper starts flying. My kids have come to call this "Mom's paper storm!" One afternoon while cleaning up after a project, I looked at a grouping of papers sitting on my desk and fell in love with the color scheme. Instantly, I knew a storm was brewing. I named this combination the five Ws because it turned out to be such a versatile look it could cover the Who, What, Where, When, and Whys of practically any occasion. Take the opportunity to let a storm of your own loose and watch what happens.

Pillow Talk: Isn't the tag closure on this little book unique? Everyone loves to open a package, and this is like unwrapping a special gift every time you untie the twill tape. There has to be a million different ways of tying these cute little books closed. What do you have sitting around the house?

ART

Artist: Pam Black
Bazzill Album: 5" x 7" Cover Alls
Album Color: Leapfrog
Binding: Fast Binding
Cardstock Color: Leapfrog
Printed Paper: BASICGREY
Rubber Stamps: Rubber Stampede
Button: Bazzill
Ink: Tsukineko, Ranger
Shipping Tags, Copper Paper Clip: Rusty Pickle
Chipboard Letters: Creative Imaginations
Bazzill Chips: Bazzill
Copper Square Studs, Copper Mini BradDots: EK Success
Film Strip: Other
Ribbons: May Arts, Other

What I Have Learned

Artist: Amy Totty
Bazzill Albums: 5" x 7" Cover Alls
Album Color: Romance
Binding: Hop, Skip, & A Jump Stitch
Cardstock Colors: Piñata
Pattern Paper: SEI
Stickers: Making Memories
Tags, Rub-Ons, Metal Tags: Making Memories
Jump Rings: Junkitz
Twill, Rick Rack, Ribbon: Fabric Store

Pillow Talk: I covered the spine of this book with patterned paper before inserting the pages. I wanted the holes in the spine to be covered since I was using a different style of binding that wouldn't be utilizing the holes. After binding it all together and pulling the twill through the slits cut into the spine, I tied knots to hold everything in place. I like to add tags or charms to the spine of the book to give it a finished look.

Pillow Talk: This beautiful little girl is a great addition to our extended family. She is the youngest grandchild and presently the only baby in our family. I cannot help but take pictures of this darling little girl every time she comes for a visit.

Ari Lynn

Artist: Amy Totty
Bazzill Album: 6" x 6" Cover Alls
Album Color: Heather
Binding: Reverse Butterfly Stitch
Magnetic Clip: Other
Button: Doodlebug Design
Rick Rack: Other
Waxed Linen: Scrapworks
Ribbon: Midori

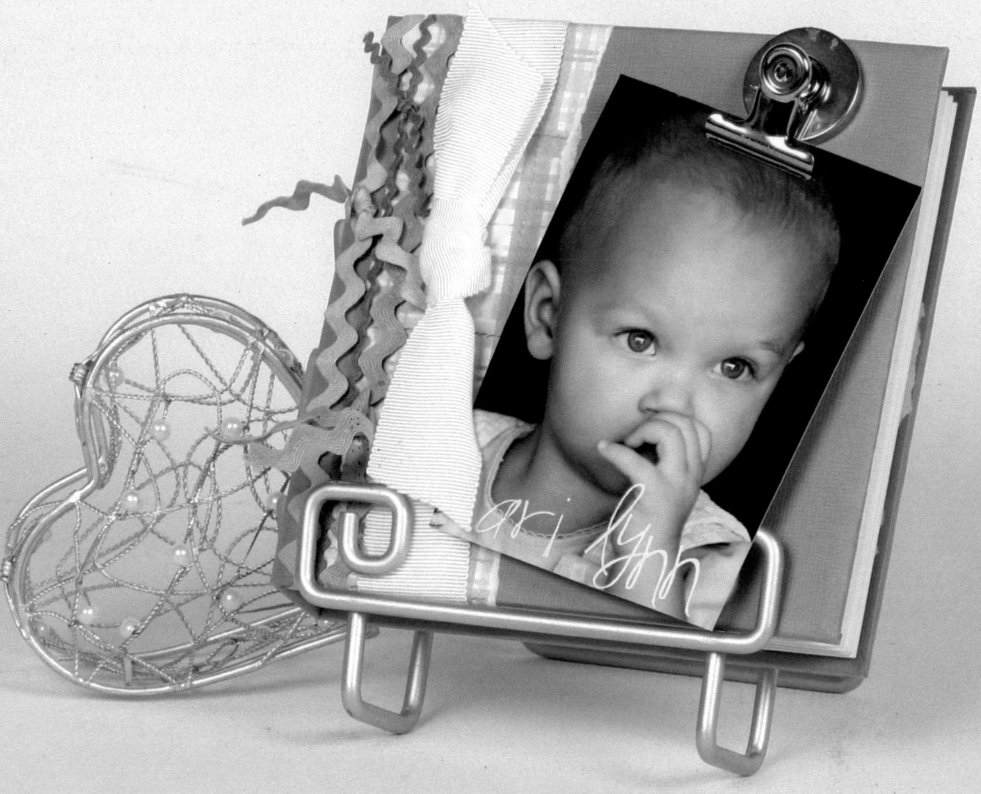

Girl Talk

Artist: Kelli Collins
Bazzill Album: 5" x 7" Mono Mini
Album Color: Jacaranda
Binding: Reverse Butterfly Stitch
Cardstock Color: Cottonwood
Bazzill Chips: Bazzill
Brads: The Happy Hammer
Printed Paper: Kangaroo & Joey
Stamps: Technique Tuesday
Ink: Tsukineko
Metal Charms: All My Memories
Waxed Linen: Other
Ribbon: Other

Pillow Talk: Add another interesting twist to your album by turning it sideways. Using Bazzill Chips, create tabs for the book that can be glued to the outer edges of the signatures. This album makes a great circle journal to exchange with friends.

going under cover

Jacob

Artist: Eva Flake
Bazzill Album: Coin Folder Album
Album Color: Bazzill White
Cardstock Colors: Lemonade/KI, Olive/KI, Pomegranate
Printed Paper: Li'l Davis Designs
Rub-Ons: Making Memories
Metal Plaque: Making Memories
Chipboard Letters: Making Memories
Color Wash: Ranger
Labels: Dymo
Sticker Phrases: Making Memories
Acrylic Paint: Making Memories
Wood Stain: JW Etc.
Measuring Tape, Safety Pins, Rick Rack, Denim Pocket, Metal Rings: Other

Pillow Talk: Pillow Talk: I created this coin folder for my son, and I wanted to make it hip and colorful. To distress the cardstock, spray orange color wash onto the Lemonade/KI cardstock to give it an orange/yellow look. Then brush aqua blue paint onto the paper for a fun finish. To age the album, brush wood stain over it. Adding the denim pocket and other accents made the coin folder really fun to look at. I cut the coin folder apart so I could re-attach it using key rings and colorful rick rack.

Pillow Talk: That's my life! I liked the idea of doing a layout about 'a day in my life'. So this is my version. I used the metal bar to hold the twill tape down so you could close the book. I loved the magnet words, but one magnet wasn't the right color so I just spray painted it to match my book. Because each of the new Bazzill albums comes with metal under the top cover, I can rearrange the magnetic words at anytime to fit my mood. I also backed each book plate with a magnet sheet, cut it to size and stuck it on the cover.

Wild & Crazy

Artist: Amy Totty
Bazzill Album: Gated Album
Album Color: Bazzill White
Binding: Fast Binding
Cardstock Colors: Teal/KI, White/KI
Buttons: Junkitz
Magnets: Other
Metal Clips: 7 gypsies
Metal Name Plate: Li'l Davis Designs
Brads: The Happy Hammer
Waxed Linen, Twill, Ribbon: Other

I Need You

Artist: Amy Totty
Bazzill Album: Gated Album
Album Color: Pomegranate
Cardstock Colors: Dark Black, White/Kl
Binding: Fast Binding
Rub-Ons: Li'l Davis Designs
Elastic, Safety Pin: Other
Ink: Tsukineko
Stencil Letters: Making Memories
Letter Stickers, Magnet Clip: Other
Pearls: ColorBök
Paint: Delta
Stamps: Making Memories
Zipper: Other
Bazzill Chips: Bazzill
Ribbon: Mokuba

Pillow Talk: The first time I heard this Leanne Rimes song on the radio I thought…that is exactly the way I feel about my honey! I know we all have busy lives and sometimes get side-tracked, but the truly important things in life need to be scrapbooked the most. You have carried me through - I need you! I love you, Todd!

Pillow Talk: To bind this album a little differently, set three silver eyelets (instead of two) on the spine. Use the reverse butterfly stitch to add the inside pages to the spine on each side of the gated album.

Live, Love, Laugh

Artist: Pam Black
Bazzill Album: Gated Album
Album Color: Maraschino
Binding: Fast Binding
Cardstock Colors: Maraschino, Route 66
Printed Papers: Chatterbox, Sweetwater
Stamps: Making Memories
Ink: Tsukineko
Leather Frame, Rub-Ons, Square Button: Making Memories
Waxy Flax: Scrapworks
Button: Junkitz
Nail Head, Silver Eyelets: American Tag
Metal Rings: Li'l Davis Designs
Laugh: Dymo
Ribbons: May Arts, Mokuba, Other

Must Be Love

Artist: Amy Totty
Bazzill Album: Zippered
Album Color: Romance
Binding: Zippered Butterfly Stitch
Pattern Paper, Stickers: SEI
Ribbon: May Arts
Stamps: Technique Tuesday
Ink: Ranger

Pillow Talk: The zippered albums go together really quick and easy. The colors and texture make it fun to play with and get creative. It can be decorated in a spectrum of ways, from simple like this one, to as complex and detailed as you want. I love to bind books with great, quality ribbon to add extra richness to such a simple binding technique.

Pillow Talk: I wanted to make my sister a gift that was a little bit different, so I color copied some old photos of the two of us as kids, and then used them in this coin folder. I like the fact that I was able to use photos that were originally taken of us together and then cut them apart. It really gives the album a "pulled together" look. There is something about old photos that is so appealing. If you can't use all the holes in the book, cover some of them up with cardstock and stamp along the bottom.

Sisters

Artist: Amy Totty
Bazzill Albums: Coin Book, Mini Mono Mini
Album Colors: Romance
Cardstock Color: Light Olive
Weave Paper: Magenta
Coin Envelope: Bazzill
Stamps, Sticker, Metal Photo Corners: Making Memories
Flowers, Elastic, Twill, Charms: Fabric Store
Paint: Delta
Image Transfer Pen: Eberhard Faber Inc.
Molding Paste: Liquitex
Rub-Ons: Making Memories

Kyle

Artist: Amy Totty
Bazzill Albums: Coin Book
Cardstock Colors: Bottleglass, Lighthouse, Lobster Bisque, Applesauce
Metal Letters: Making Memories
Label: Dymo
Stickers: Making Memories
Chipboard Letters: Li'l Davis Designs
Magic Cards: Wizards of the Coast
Yugio Cards: Konami
Black Metal Letters: Other
Rub-Ons: Li'l Davis Designs

Pillow Talk: Good ol' Kyle. My 11 year-old is a great kid! Kyle is a lot like his oldest brother Kevin and they do so many activities together. In a family as large as our, sometimes it feels like all the kids get lumped together in photos and books. I really wanted to showcase Kyle in a special way so that he could see just how special he is to me. I think Kyle knows it; he has already cleared a spot on the shelf in his room for this album.

Pillow Talk: I wanted to record the entire process of building our house and watching it transform into our new home; so creating an album with a homespun look seemed the perfect way to carry on the theme. To age the cover, sand the patterned paper until the white finish peeks through. Rake the brown ink pad across the side and front of the album. To give it a finished look, use wood stain to paint over the cover.

Our New Home

Artist: Eva Flake
Bazzill Album: Gated Album
Album Color: Walnut
Binding: Fast Binding
Cardstock Colors: Brick Road
Printed Paper: Chatterbox
Stamps: Making Memories, Other
Ink: Ranger
Acrylic Paint: Delta
Buttons: Bazzill
Ribbon: May Arts
Brads: All My Memories
Wood Stain: JW Etc.
Buckle, Twill Tape: Other

Kevin

Artist: Amy Totty
Bazzill Album: Zippered
Album Color: Typhoon
Binding: Fast Binding
Color Wash: Ranger
Tiles: Deluxe Designs
Barcode: Mystic Press
Chain, Black Twill: Other

Pillow Talk: This is a classic Kevin day…headphones on, playing on the computer or watching TV. Oh, the life of a 16 year-old! He really is a great kid, no complaints here! I tried to keep this book simple by using chain to hold the pages in the book. I feel this gives the book a masculine look, but still keeps it feeling fun.

Pillow Talk: Do you realize The Bazzill Basics Paper albums have metal in between the cover and the paper so it can be decorated with magnets? I added a sheet of metal on the middle set of cut out circles so I could make a tic-tac-toe board. This makes a great traveling game for my kids. I decided to make the game board more flexible by cutting the album apart at the seams and then reattaching each side with hook tape and tying with rick rack for extra durability. I plan to make one for each of my kids before our next road trip to Grandma's house.

Travel Fun

Artist: Amy Totty
Bazzill Album: Coin
Album Color: Pomegranate
Cardstock Colors: Apricot, Teal/Kl
Stencil, Rub-Ons: Making Memories
Stamps: Other
Ink: Tsukineko
Bottle Caps, Hook Tape, Rick Rack: Other

My Life

Artist: Kelli Collins
Bazzill Album: Coin
Album Color: Cottonwood
Bosher, Bazzill Chips: Bazzill
Brads: All My Memories, The Happy Hammer
Printed Paper: Basic Grey, K & Co.
Metal Key Hole, Text Tiles, Acrylic Frame: The Creative Block
Stickers: All My Memories
Mailbox Number, Paper Tag, Rub-On Words, Small Safety Pin: Making Memories
Letter Beads: Westrim Crafts
Tags: EK Success
Metal Charm: Art Chix
Transparency: Creative Imaginations
Metal Frame: Coffee Break Design
Twill Tape, Old Post Card, Tape Measure Pieces, Clip, Metal Findings, Game Pieces, Rick Rack, Ribbons, Bottle Cap, Buttons, Silk Flower: Other

Pillow Talk: When creating a coin album, don't limit yourself to placing objects inside the precut circles. Create great visual appeal by adding square and rectangle objects to cover up some of the holes, and don't be afraid to let embellishments extend over the edge of the album. This album doubles as a photo frame that stands open on a shelf or counter.

Pillow Talk: I wanted to make a gated album with the hop, skip, & a jump stitch because it is my favorite binding. To make this book, follow the directions in the how-to section, except add one more piece of twill. This middle piece of twill is sewn over like the middle stitch in the sample. The gated album comes with four signatures, so for this book I took two of the signatures and made an additional binding on the other side of the book. This makes the book look elegant because the pages open in opposite directions.

BéBe

Artist: Amy Totty
Bazzill Album: Gated
Album Color: Heather
Binding: Hop, Skip, & A Jump
Pattern Paper: me & my big ideas
Rub-Ons: Making Memories
Safety Pin, Rick Rack: Other
Ribbon: Other

Museum of Totty Art

Artist: Amy Totty
Bazzill Album: Gated Album
Album Color: Bazzill White
Binding: Fast Binding
Cardstock Colors: Dark Black, White/KI
Pattern Paper: KI Memories
Stamp: Technique Tuesday
Ink: Tsukineko
Stickers: Making Memories
Brads: The Happy Hammer
Metal Case, Handles, Magnetic Clip: Other
Waxed Linen: Other

Pillow Talk: Doesn't everyone have a refrigerator filled with a priceless collection of art made by their children? I can't bring myself to throw any of this away, so I came up with my own way to preserve these fine pieces of art. I created a book to resemble a refrigerator by attaching handles to the cover with brads. I added the lining before installing the handles for extra reinforcement. I bound the book and filled the inside with the greatest creations made so far by the Totty family artists.

WE'VE GOTCHA
COVERED

Friendship

Artist: Kelli Collins
Bazzill Album: 5" x 7" Mono Mini
Album Color: Dark Violet
Bosher: Bazzill
Color Wash Ink: Ranger
Jump Ring: Junkitz
Sticker: O Scrap!
Flower, Decorative Brad, Silver Brad, Word Tiles, Safety Pin, Metal Word Charm: Making Memories
Plaid Ribbon: Offray
Chain, Safety Pin, Elastic, Ribbon, and Flower Bead: Other

Pillow Talk: Alter the color of your album by spraying on the Color Wash and applying the ink by dragging the stamp pad (direct-to-paper method) across the surface in a hit or miss fashion, until the desired color is achieved.

Pillow Talk: This book has a little bit of a "shabby-chic" look to it because there are so many different embellishments. The thing that makes it so appealing is the cottage feel of the color scheme. Red and aqua are some of the new color ways making a big comeback.

Love

Artist: Pam Black
Bazzill Album: 6" x 6" Mono Mini
Album Color: Pomegranate
Cardstock Colors: Pomegranate, Pinecone
Printed Paper: Daisy D's
Stamps: Hero Arts
Ink: Ranger
Photo Turn, Safety Pin, Decorative Brad, Chipboard Stencil Letter: Making Memories
Silk Flower: Other
Heart Punch: Emagination
Rub-Ons: Li'l Davis Designs
Paper Clip: 7gypsies
Antique Mini-Brad: American Tag
Bazzill Chips: Bazzill
Button: SEI
Ribbons: May Arts, Other
RickRack: Other

Birthday Calendar

Artist: Amy Totty
Bazzill Album: Mega Mono Mini
Album Color: Pink
Cardstock Color: Piñata, Fresh, Teal/Kl
Pattern Paper: SEI
Tabs: SEI
Rick Rack: Other
Ribbon: May Arts
Rub-Ons: Autumn Leaves

Pillow Talk: I don't know about you, but I can never keep track of anyone's birthday. So I thought it would be fun to make a birthday calendar where I could record not just the dates of birthdays of friends or family, but also keep track of their favorite things. I will be organized some day and this is one cute way to start.

Pillow Talk: I created this album for my niece, who was born this past summer. I decorated the cover to match her nursery so that her mother can display her special album for all to see.

Emma

Artist: Eva Flake
Bazzill Album: 8" x 8" Post
Album Color: Baby Pink
Foam Stamps: Making Memories
Button: Bazzill
Ribbon: May Arts
Acrylic Paint: Delta
Foam Stamp, Silk Flower, Fiber, and Rick
Rack: Other

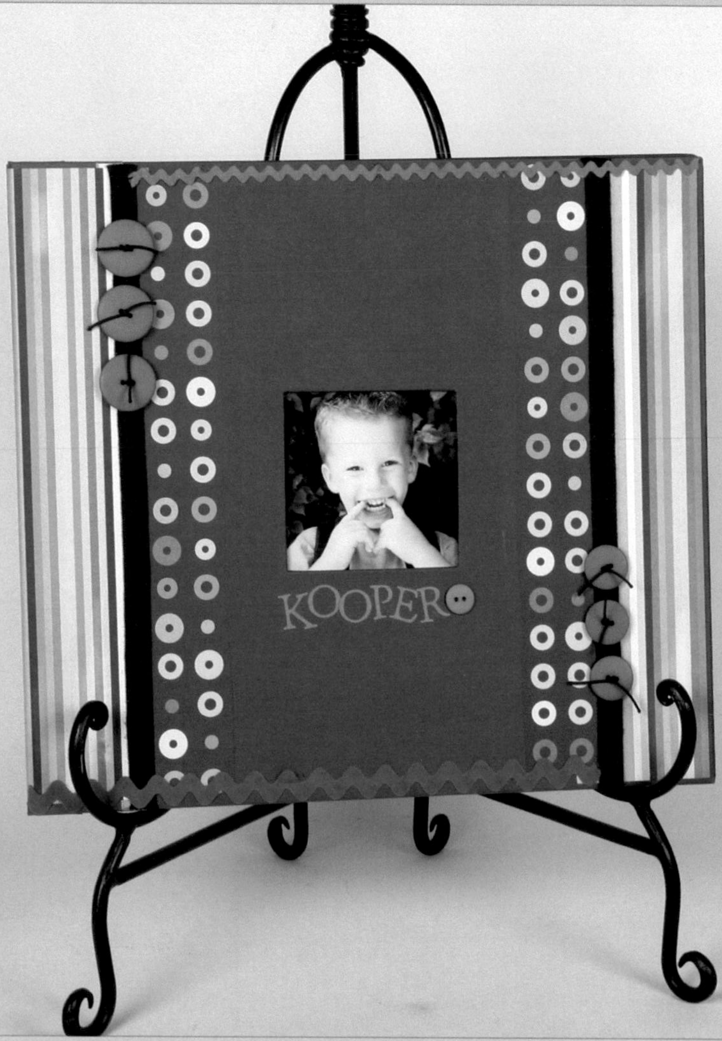

Kooper

Artist: Amy Totty
Bazzill Album: 12" x 12" Post
Album Color: Typhoon
Cardstock Color: Olive/KI
Pattern Paper: KI Memories
Letters: Quickutz - Paige
Buttons: Junkitz
Rick Rack, Elastic, Ribbon: Other

Pillow Talk: Our four year-old, Kooper, is our youngest child and by far, he is certainly the most independent. After watching his three older brothers and sister do so many things for themselves, he just doesn't understand why he can't. We discovered this when we walked into the kitchen to find he had gotten waffles out of the freezer, toasted them, plated them, grabbed the syrup, and was enjoying freshly cooked waffles. When we asked what he thought he was doing, he simply stated, "Eatin' waffles."

Pillow Talk: When the waxed linen is on the outside of the book try stringing beads, charms, or buttons on before stitching it to the book. This is a chance to add variety and an extra special touch to your book. Have fun with it!

Back to School

Artist: Amy Totty
Bazzill Album: 6" x 6" Cover Alls
Album Color: Pomegranate
Binding: Reverse Butterfly Stitch
Cardstock Color: Hillary
Printed Paper: Daisy D's
Rub-On: Making Memories
Jump Rings: Junkitz
Brads: Making Memories
D Rings, Beads, Charms, Elastic, Metal Ring: Other

Laugh Out Loud

Artist: Amy Totty
Bazzill Album: 6" x 6" Mono Mini
Album Color: Dark Black
Cardstock Colors: Piñata
Pattern Paper: BASICGREY
Black Frame: Pressed Petals
Large and Small Rick Rack: Other
Safety Pins, Elastic: Other
Grommet Twill: Other
Ribbon: May Arts

Those who laugh without cause have either found the true meaning of happiness or have gone stark raving mad.

Pillow Talk: I loved this black frame and thought it would be so cute to frame a Mono Mini in it. Line the frame with pattern paper and then mat the 6" x 6" Mono Mini on the frame. This makes such a great gift that can sit on a shelf or desk filled with pictures and stories that are close to that special someone's heart.

Pillow Talk: Doesn't it seem like we NEVER have enough time! Let this cute little book remind you to "make time" for the people and the things you love in your life. Use a printed transparency over patterned paper for a different look, making sure to secure it to the front, hidden under an embellishment so you can't see where it has been attached.

Make Time

Artist: Pam Black
Bazzill Album: 8" x 8" Mono Mini
Album Color: Dark Olive
Cardstock Color: Dark Olive
Printed Paper: K & Company
Transparency: K & Company
Ink: Ranger
Fonts: 2Peas - Evergreen
Jumbo Silver Brads, Decorative Brad: Making Memories
Twill Tape: Unknown
Paper Flower: Prima
Metal Screen: Scrap Yard
Clear Tabs, Staples: Office Supply Store
Paint: Deco Art, Lamp Black
Ribbon: May Arts

My Journal

Artist: Amy Totty
Bazzill Album: 6" x 6" Cover Alls
Album Color: Pomegranate
Binding: Reverse Butterfly Stitch
Book Tape: Making Memories
Hook Tape: Other
Ribbon: May Arts

Pillow Talk: This book was refreshing to make. I wanted to have a journal to write down my thoughts and feelings in, but wanted the look to be clean and simple. I bound the book using the butterfly stitch on the inside using waxed linen. I used black hook tape to cover the stitches and the spine so I could run ribbon through it as a closure for the journal.

Pillow Talk: This album was so simple and fast to put together. The stickers integrate so well with the color and the theme I was shooting for. The look was so clean and crisp that it didn't require much more to complete it. The stickers came in lots of great colors and themes. The ease of these makes it simple for you to create a beautiful gift for someone in a snap.

My Family

Artist: Amy Totty
Bazzill Album: 8" x 8" Post
Album Color: Leapfrog
Ink: Technique Tuesday
Stickers: Making Memories
Twill: Other

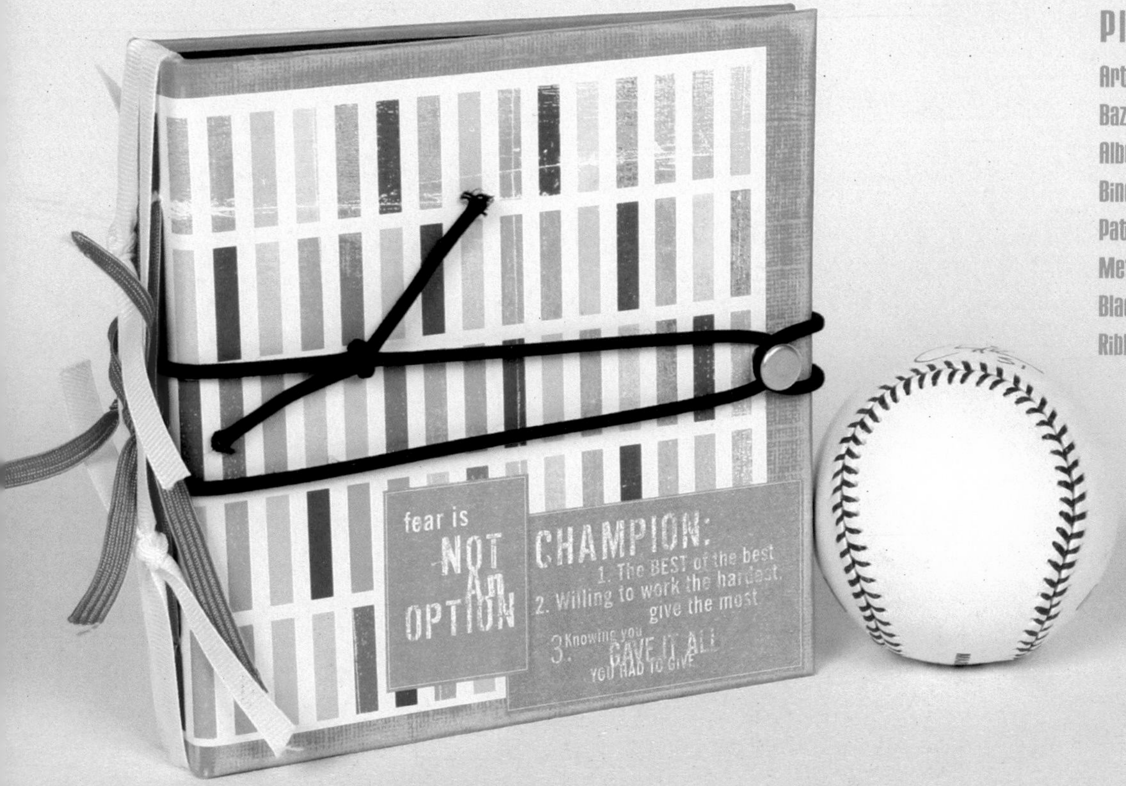
fear is
NOT
An
OPTION
CHAMPION:
1. The BEST of the best
2. Willing to work the hardest,
give the most
3. Knowing you
GAVE IT ALL
YOU HAD TO GIVE

Play

Artist: Amy Totty
Bazzill Album: 6" x 6" Cover Alls
Album Color: Jacaranda
Binding: Ribbon Over Spine & Fast Binding
Pattern Paper: BASICGREY
Metal Post, Stickers: Making Memories
Black Elastic, Orange Trim: Other
Ribbon: Offray

Pillow Talk: I chose to use ribbon as the binding material for sewing the signatures on the cover. There are so many neat things like ribbon, elastic, twill, or fibers to sew the signatures in, use your imagination and have fun.

Pillow Talk: Now that I am an adult and have children of my own, I really treasure my friendship with my Mom. I wanted to make a book about the things that I admire most about her and the things that make our friendship such a treasure to me. I am so grateful to have such an incredible confidant, whom I can also call Mom! In this book, the Mono Mini is already bound, so to create a more elegant look I chose to take out the staples and use a butterfly stitch through the spine to rebind it.

Mom

Artist: Amy Totty
Bazzill Album: 6" x 6" Mono Mini
Album Color: Dark Olive
Binding: Butterfly Stitch
Cardstock: Dark Butter
Pattern Paper: Chatterbox
Ink: Ranger
Brads: All My Memories
Safety Pin: Dritz
Chenille Rick Rack, Waxed Linen: Other
Stamps: Technique Tuesdays

Friends

Artist: Kelli Collins
Bazzill Album: 6" x 6" Cover Alls
Album Color: Pomegranate
Binding: Ribbon Over Spine
Large Die-Cut Initial: my mind's eye
Label: Dymo
Magnetic Photo Frame: Other
Elastic Hair Bands: Goody
Rick Rack, Elastic, Ribbons: Other

Pillow Talk: Disregard the holes in the spine when binding this album. Instead, cut the metal piece from elastic hair bands and use these colorful hair accessories to tie your signatures to the spine. While Bazzill Basics Paper albums look great decorated with lots of stuff, don't be afraid to orchestrate a simple look by adding only a few embellishments.

Pillow Talk: It's amazing what a difference a year can make. I have found it to be a great learning experience to create a book like this, each year around my birthday. In it I take the opportunity to look back on the previous year and record some of the times that stick out most in my memory. I also take the chance to record my gratitude, frustrations, joys, and lows for the year. I also include any goals, or things I would like to focus on for the coming year. It can be very enlightening to review these each year and can show how different influences in your life can mold you.

What a Year

Artist: Amy Totty
Bazzill Album: 6" x 6" Mono Mini
Album Color: Dark Sand
Cardstock Colors: Dark Olive, Dark Chocolate, Dark Butter, Dark Scarlet
Pattern Paper: Chatterbox
Bazzill Chips: Bazzill
Tabs: Accu Cut
Ink: Ranger
Stamps: Technique Tuesday
Ribbon: May Arts

Pillow Talk: I love Christmas! What a great time to slow down and spend more time with your family. Growing up, we always had advent calendars filled with chocolate or candy to help us with the anticipation of the holiday. I thought it would be fun to have a calendar that instead of giving candy each day, had a variety of things listed that our family could do to help encourage the holiday spirit. Our advent calendar includes everything from listing great Christmas recipes for the family to make together to listing names of books to snuggle up and read together. One thing that we always include in each year's calendar is a small service project that can be done with our children. This is such an excellent way to celebrate the season!

Advent Calendar

Artist: Amy Totty
Bazzill Album: 6" x 6" Mono Mini, Mini Mono Minis
Album Color: Dark Olive, Pomegranate, Dark Sand
Cardstock Colors: Olive/Kl, Travertine, Pomegranate, Dark Olive, Dark Sand, Hillary
Stamps: Making Memories
Paint: Delta
Ink: Ranger
Charms: Pressed Petals
Bottle Caps, Stencils: Li'l Davis Designs
Safety Pins, Thick Book Board, Hinges, Brads: Other
Metal Clip: 7 gypsies
Metal Zip Pulls: Pebbles Inc.
Small and Large Rick Rack: Other
Ribbon: May Arts, Offray, Midori
Name Plates: Accu Cut
Jump Ring: Junkitz

Feeling Groovy

Artist: Amy Totty
Bazzill Album: 5" x 7" Mono Mini
Album Color: Dark Chocolate
Cardstock Colors: Dark Olive, Light Chocolate, Dark Chocolate
Pattern Paper: Chatterbox
Bazzill Chips: Bazzill
Velcro, Safety Pin, Wide Twill: Other
Jump Ring: Junkitz

Pillow Talk: The straps that wrap around this mono mini are made out of cardstock. Isn't that an easy idea? Just glue each piece down in the back and then fold it to the front. Use hook and loop as the fastener for the straps. Add the look of buttons by covering Bazzill Chips with cardstock and then cutting around each one.

the Big cover up

Decisions, Decisions, Decisions,

There are so many different ways to finish the inside of a book. Begin by deciding if you want to:

1. Use only the pages included in the book.
2. Use the existing pages included with the book, but add a few more.
3. Completely replace all the pages in the book with as many pages and the type of paper you want.

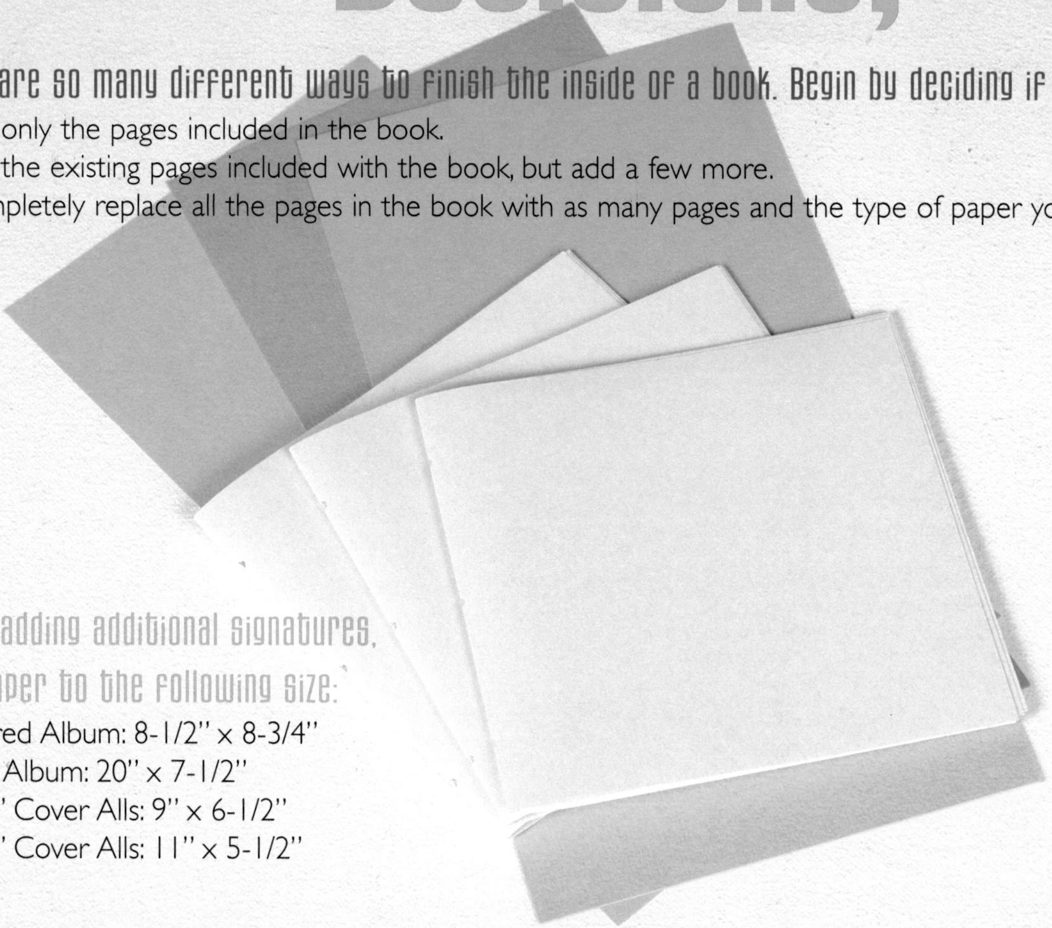

When adding additional signatures, cut paper to the following size:

Zippered Album: 8-1/2" x 8-3/4"
Gated Album: 20" x 7-1/2"
5" x 7" Cover Alls: 9" x 6-1/2"
6" x 6" Cover Alls: 11" x 5-1/2"

Creating More Signatures

1. Score and fold pages in half. Slip one page inside the other until all of the sheets nest together. There should be no more than three pages nested together at a time.
2. Match up the signature with the holes in the paper included with the album, and using an awl or needle, pierce through all layers of paper. Add as many additional signatures as you like using this same technique.

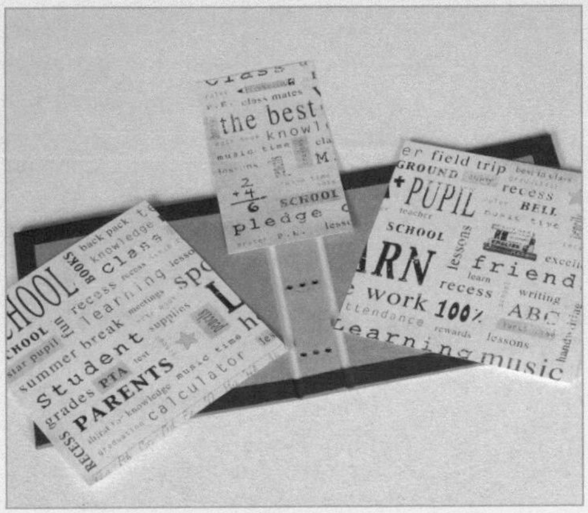

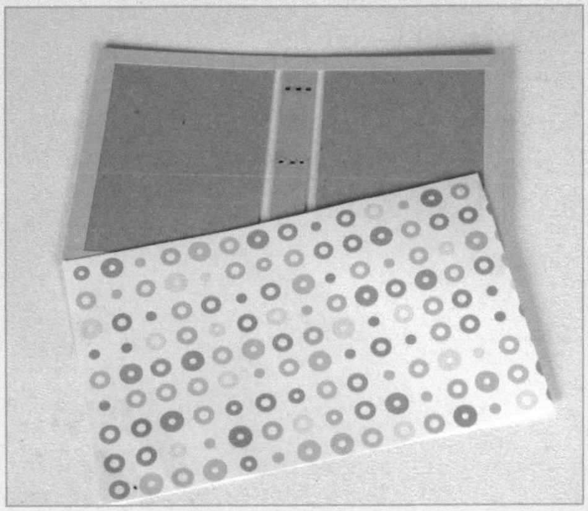

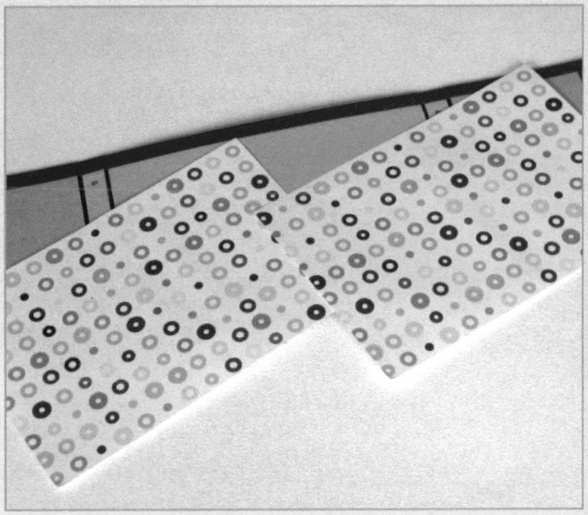

Lining the 6" x 6" Cover Alls:

Cut two 5-1/2" x 5-3/4" pieces and one 3" x 5-3/4" piece of printed paper or cardstock. Use the large pieces to line the inside front and back covers. Position the smaller piece over the spine, overlapping onto the front and back lining pieces. Adhere with glue, using a brayer to secure.

Lining the 5" x 7" Cover Alls:

Cut one 10-3/4" x 6-3/4" piece of printed paper or cardstock to use as a liner inside the front and back covers. Position liner and adhere with glue, using a brayer to secure.

Lining the Gated Album:

Cut two 7-1/2" x 11" pieces of printed paper or cardstock to use as a liner inside the front and back covers; the ends of the paper will butt together. Adhere with glue, using a brayer to secure.

Lining the Zippered Album:

Cut two 4-1/4" x 8-3/4" pieces and one 1" x 8" piece of printed paper. Position the larger pieces of paper over the unfinished areas on the front and back covers. This size is cut to show the zigzag stitching. Use the small strip to cover the spine of the book. Adhere with glue, using a brayer to secure.

ALWAYS add the lining first, before inserting any of the pages. If you're going to cover the outside of the book with any additional paper, be sure to cover the outside spine BEFORE inserting the inside liner.

Adding Eyelets

If adding eyelets in predrilled holes, mark liner using a pencil and make a large hole with an Anywhere Hole Punch or Japanese Screw Punch. Using an eyelet setter, insert eyelets in pre-drilled holes. Standard size eyelets will fit in these holes, but may leave an unfinished edge on the inside spine.

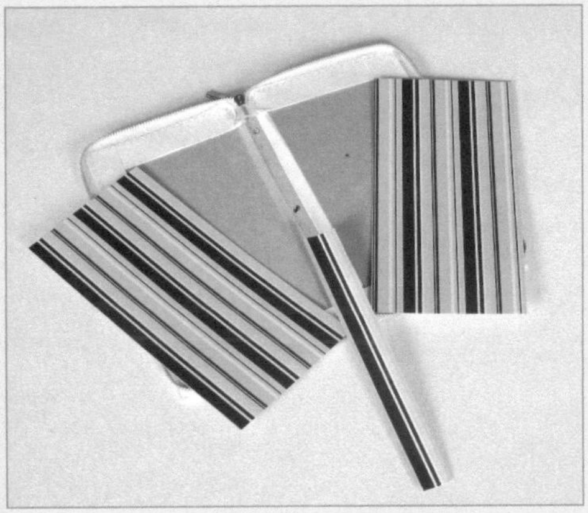

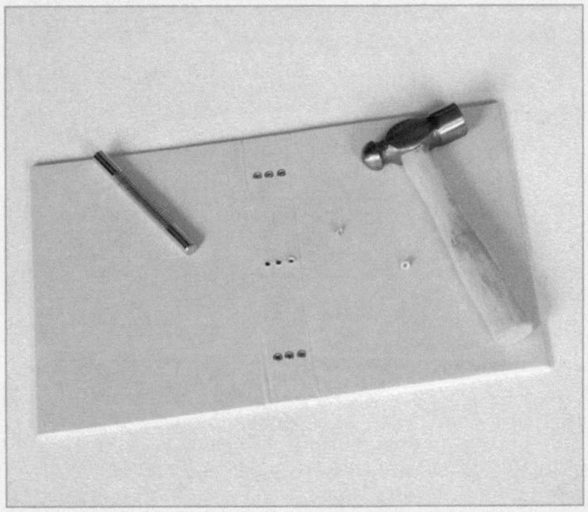

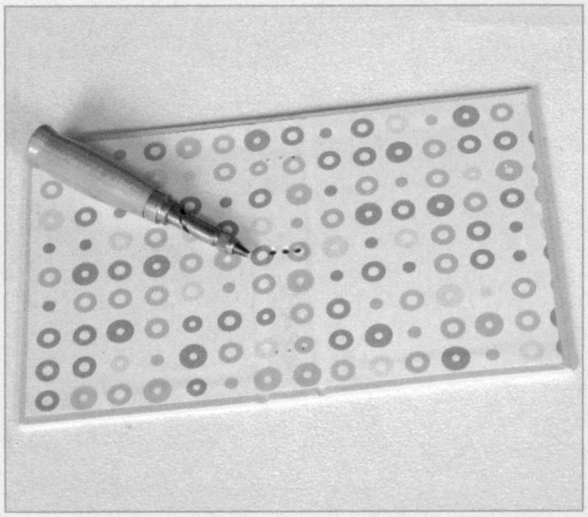

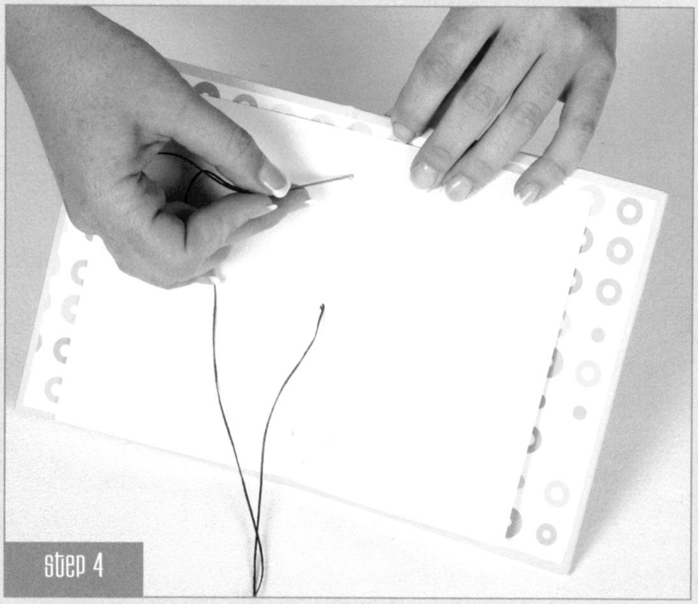

1. Thread a needle with 36" of waxed linen thread. More thread will be needed later.

2. To begin stitching book together, match up signature holes with the holes in the cover.

3. Leaving a 2" tail, insert the needle through the middle hole of the spine and out through the middle hole of each page in the signature, ending inside the book.

4. Insert needle into the top hole in the signature and through the top hole in the spine, ending outside the book.

5. Insert needle in the bottom hole in the signature and through the bottom hole in the spine, ending inside the book.

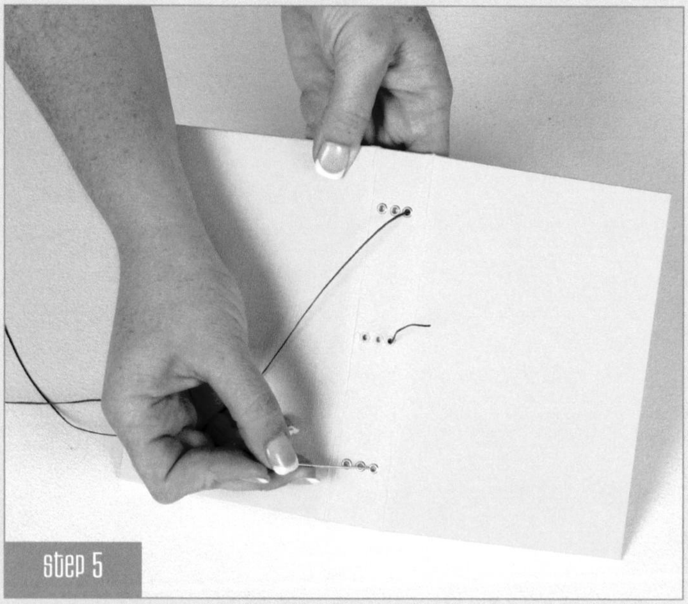

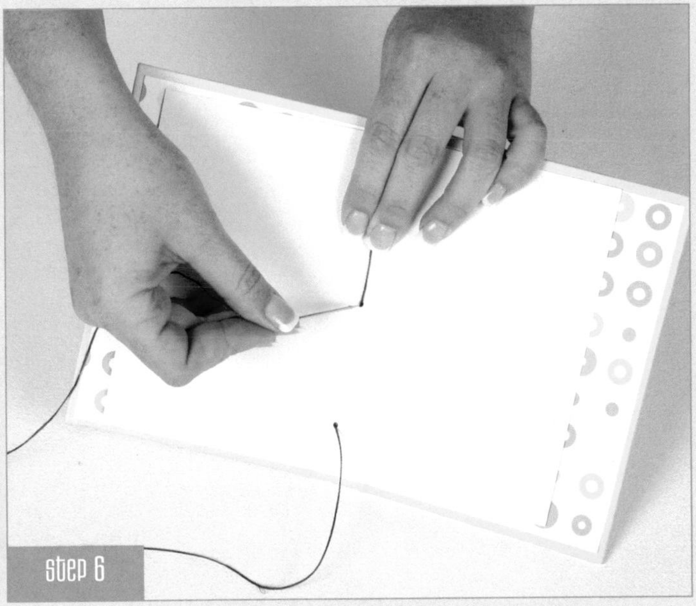

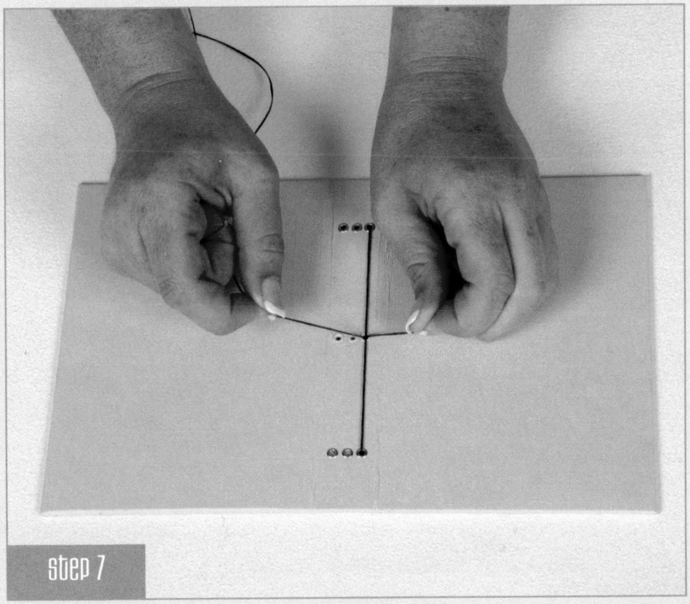

6. Finish by inserting needle back into the middle hole in the signature and back through the middle hole in the spine.

7. Pull the ends of the waxed linen taut; making sure each end of the waxed linen is on opposite sides of the piece of linen that runs down the middle of the book. The middle string will be tied down. Tie a knot.

Butterfly Stitch

This stitch is great for binding Bazzill Basic Paper's Cover Alls.

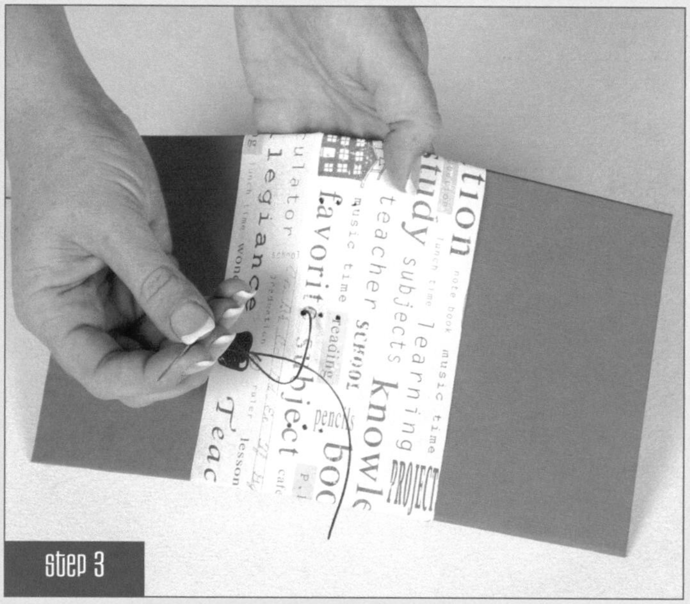

step 3

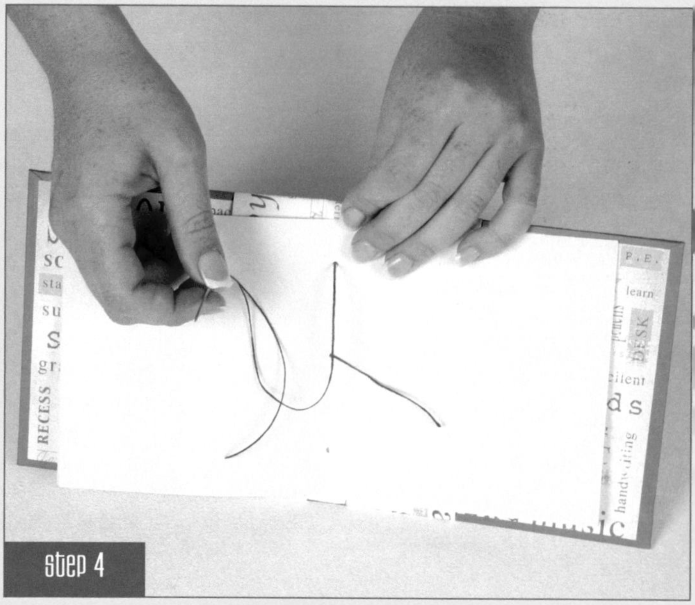

step 4

1. Thread a needle with 36" of waxed linen thread. More thread will be needed later.

2. To begin stitching book together, match up signature holes with the holes in the cover.

3. Leaving a 2" tail, insert the needle through the middle hole of each page in the signature and then out through the middle hole of the spine, ending outside the book.

4. Insert needle into the top hole in the spine and through the top hole in the signature, ending inside the book.

5. Insert needle in the bottom hole in the signature and through the bottom hole in the spine, ending outside the book.

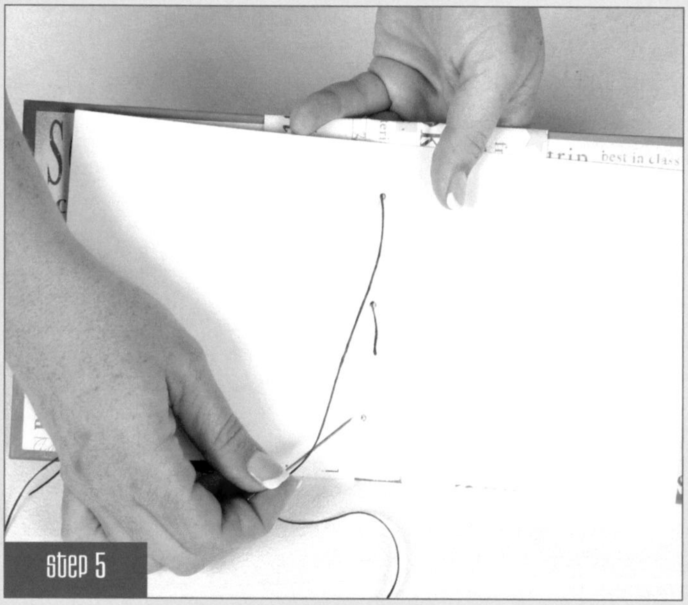

step 5

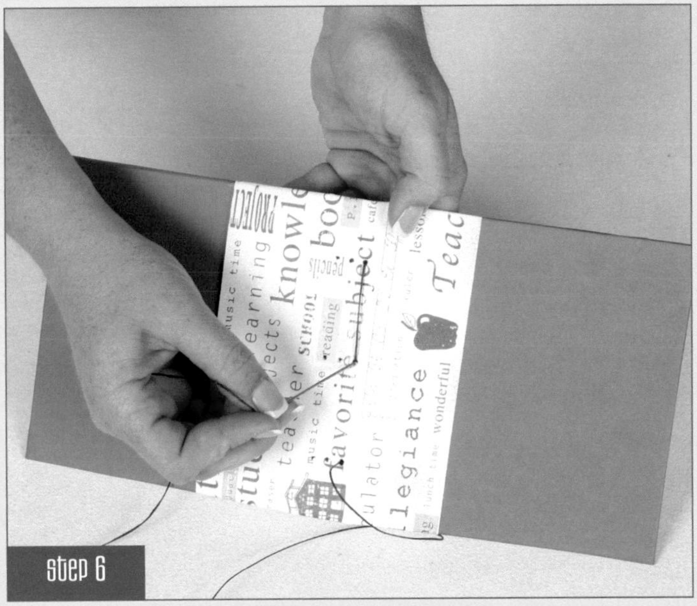
step 6

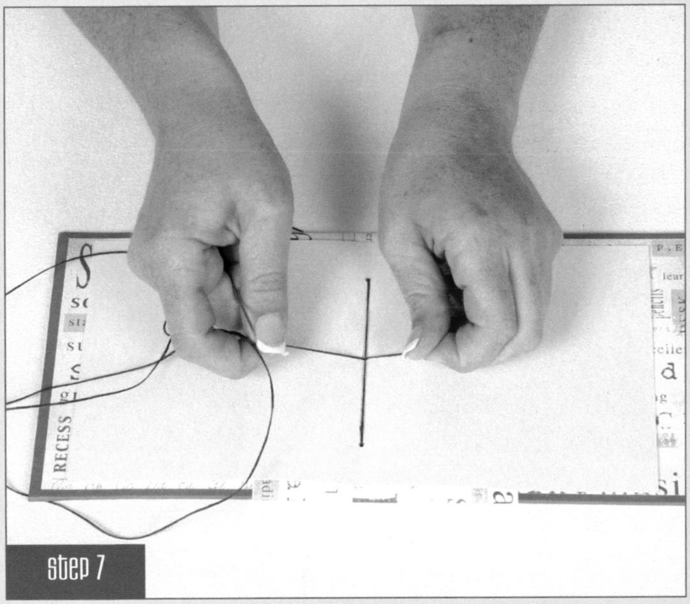
step 7

6. Finish by inserting needle back into the middle hole in the spine and back through the middle hole in the signature.

7. Pull the ends of the waxed linen taut; making sure each end of the waxed linen is on opposite sides of the piece of linen that runs down the middle of the book. The middle string will be tied down. Tie a knot.

Reverse Butterfly Stitch

This stitch is great for binding Bazzill Basic Paper's Cover Alls.

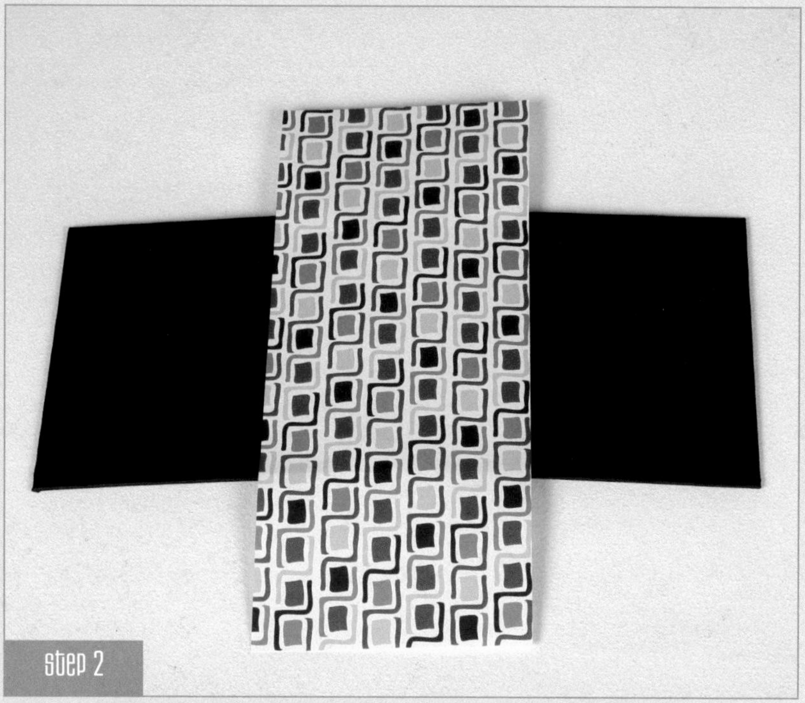
step 2

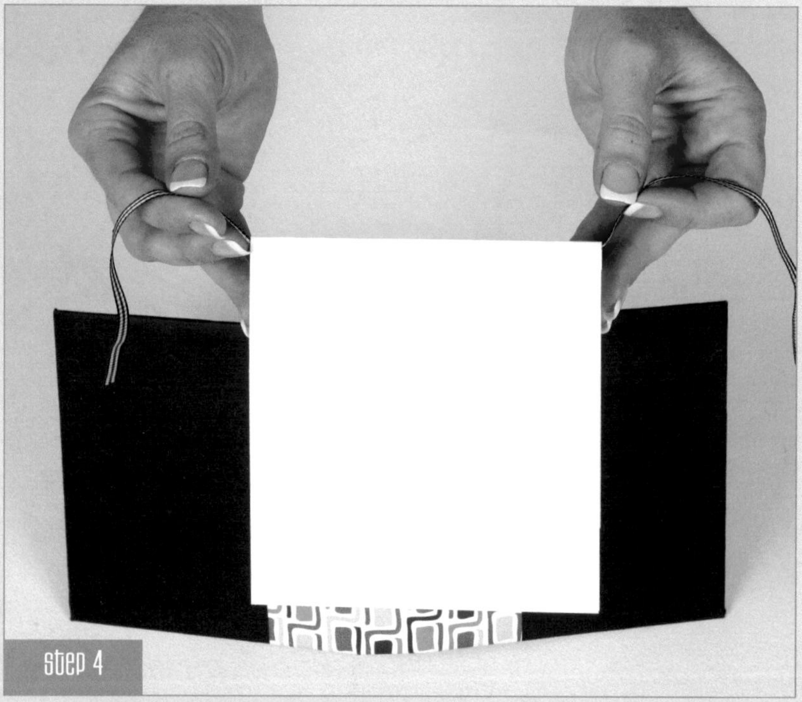
step 4

Ribbon Over Spine:

This is a great way to cover the spine of any of Bazzill Basics Paper's new albums.

Before beginning, cover the outside of the book with additional paper. You don't want the holes in the spine to show. When using the Ribbon Over Spine technique, be sure to add the liner before adding the signatures to the book.

1. Cover the predrilled holes along the spine of the book with a strip of cardstock or patterned paper. The strip can be any width, but no longer than 12".

2. Find the center of the paper strip and position it along the spine. Fold the top and bottom edges over the edge of the book. Glue in place and use a brayer to secure. Add the remaining liner pieces.

3. Cut an 18" piece of ribbon (if tying in a knot) or 28" piece of ribbon (if tying a bow) for each signature being added to the book.

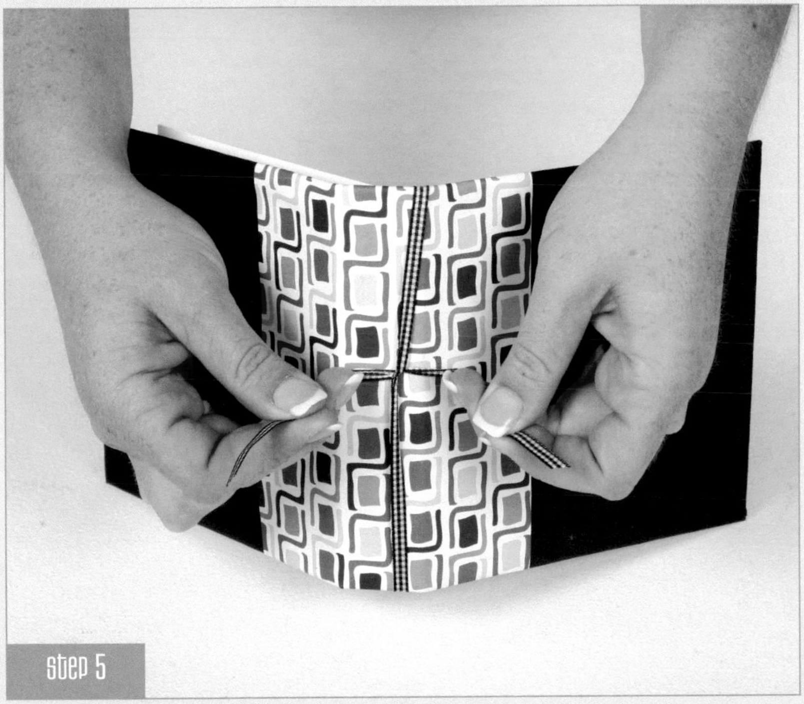

step 5

4. Find the center of one piece of ribbon and place it along the inside fold of one signature.

5. Position the signature into the Cover Alls with the fold against the inside spine.
Wrap the ribbon around to the outside of book. Pull ribbon taut against the spine, double knot. Tie a bow, if there is enough ribbon remaining.

6. Place another signature inside the book, next to the first one. Continue securing each signature with more ribbon

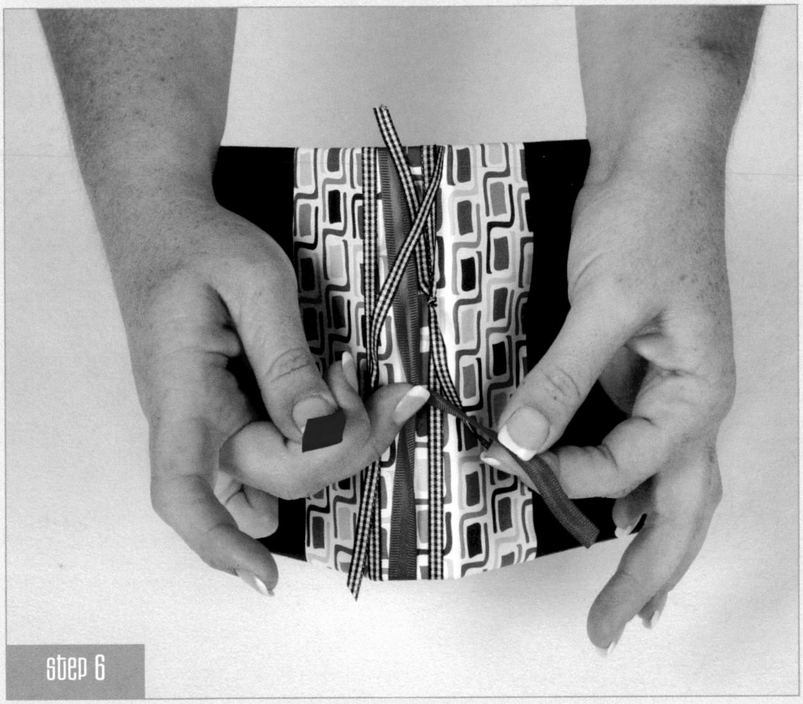

step 6

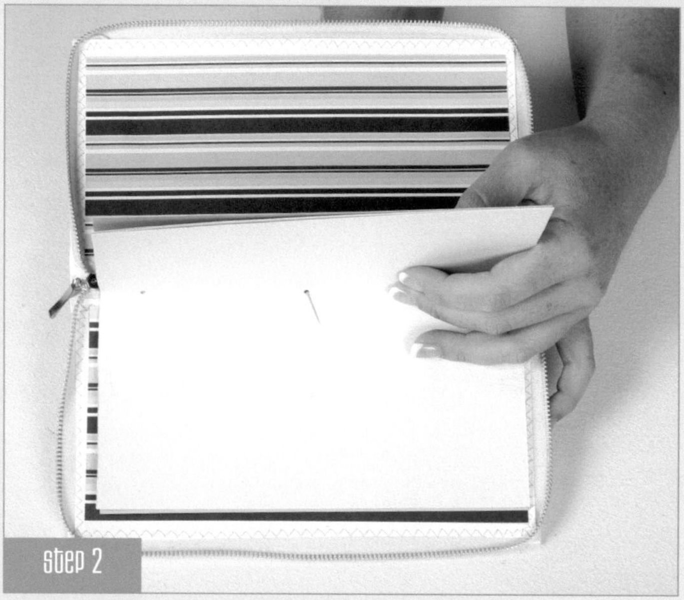

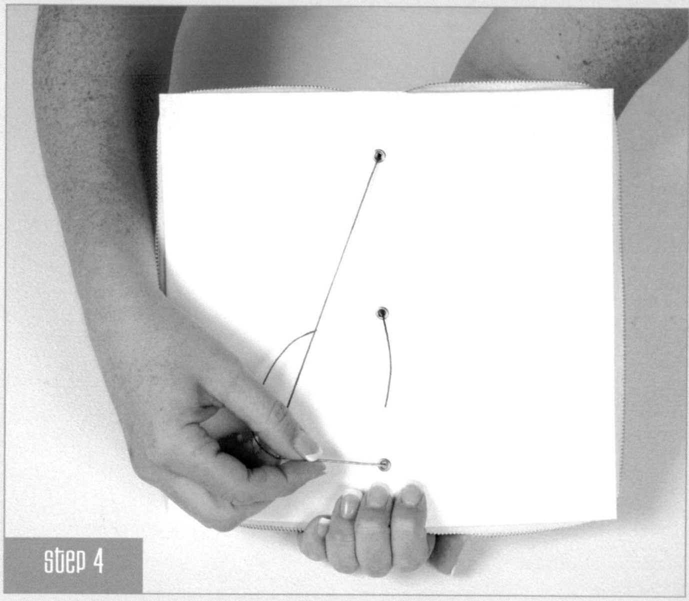

Zippered Butterfly Stitch

This stitch is great for binding Bazill Basics Paper's Zippered Album. Try it using twill, ribbon, crochet thread, or any other fiber. You can start stitching from the inside or the outside, your pick.

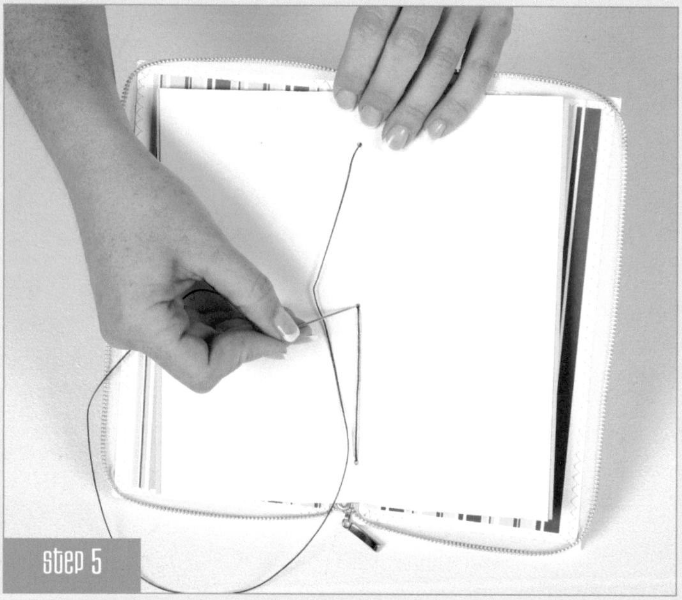

1. Thread a needle with 36" of waxed linen thread.

2. Leaving a 2" tail, insert the needle through the middle hole of the spine and then out through the middle hole of the signature, ending inside the book.

3. Insert needle into the top hole of the signature and through the top hole of the spine, ending outside the book.

4. Insert needle in the bottom hole in the spine and through the bottom hole in the signature, ending inside the book.

5. Finish by inserting needle back into the middle hole in the signature and back through the middle hole in the spine.

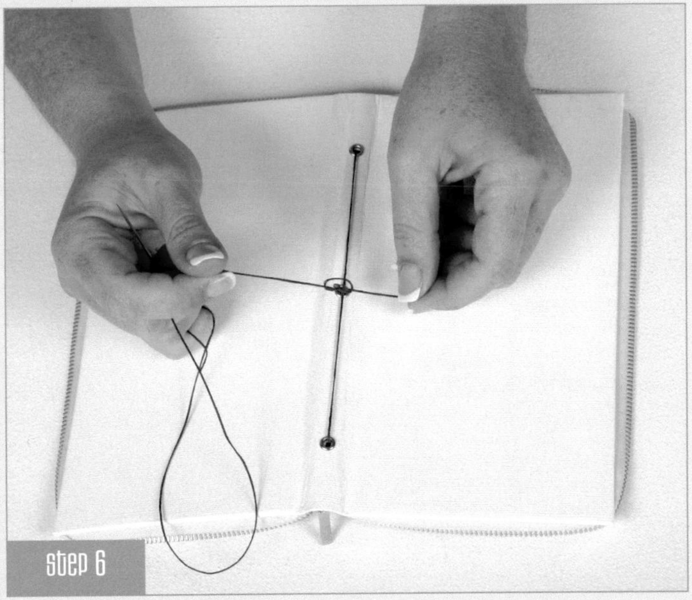

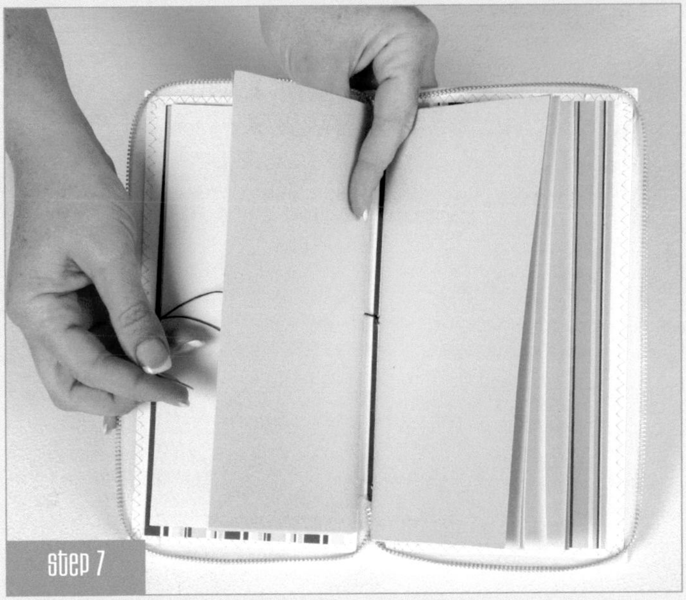

6. Pull the ends of the waxed linen taut; making sure each end of the waxed linen is on opposite sides of the piece of linen that runs down the middle of the book. The middle string will be tied down. Tie a knot.

7. Be sure to match up holes in signature on either side of the zipper in the spine. If the zipper is in the way, carefully cut off the tail.

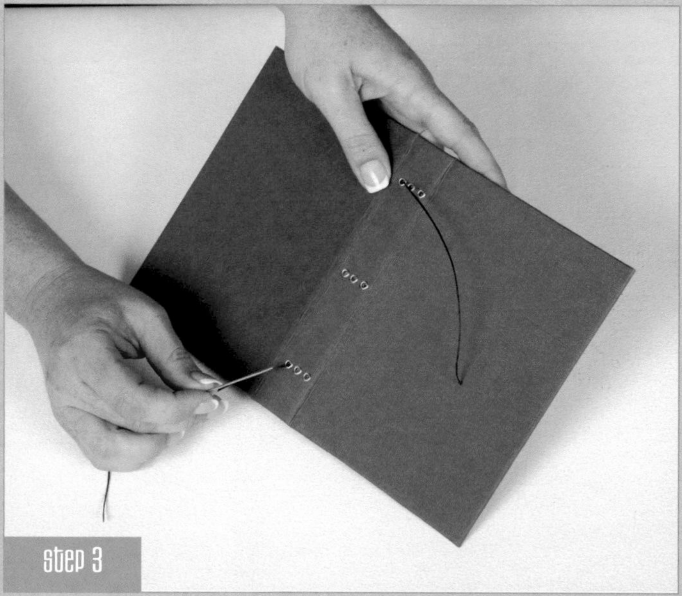

1. Thread a needle with 36" of waxed linen thread. More thread will be needed later.

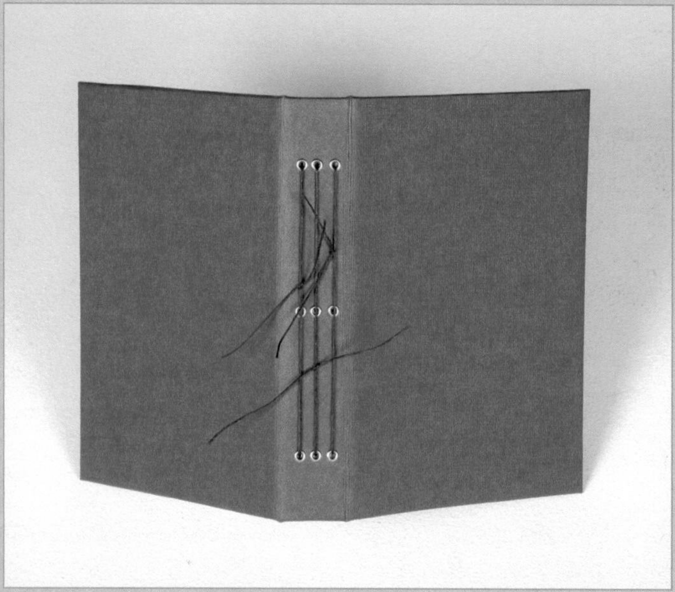

2. To begin stitching book together, match up signature holes with the holes in the spine on the left side of the cover.

3. Leaving an 8" tail, insert the needle through the top hole of the spine and then through the top hole of each signature, ending inside the book. Insert the needle into the bottom hole of the signature and out through the bottom hole of the spine, ending outside the book.

4. Pull the ends of the waxed linen taut and tie a knot.

5. When adding signatures to the Gated Album, be sure to begin working from the left side and then alternate to the right side when adding signatures.

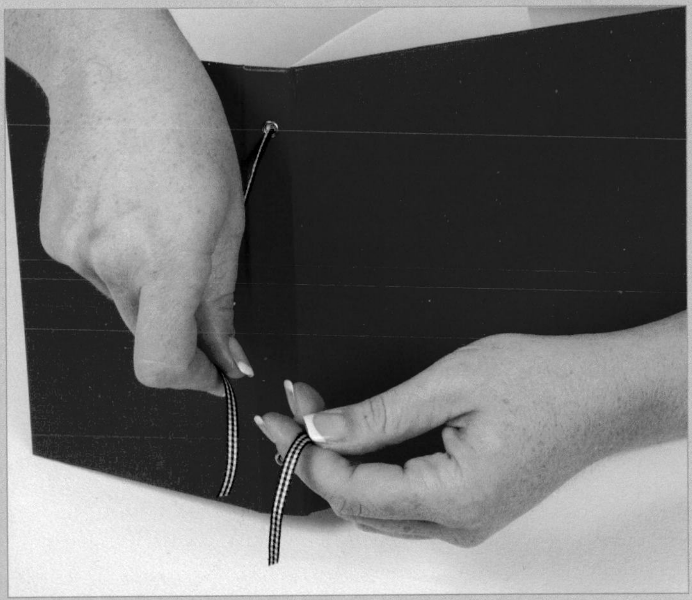

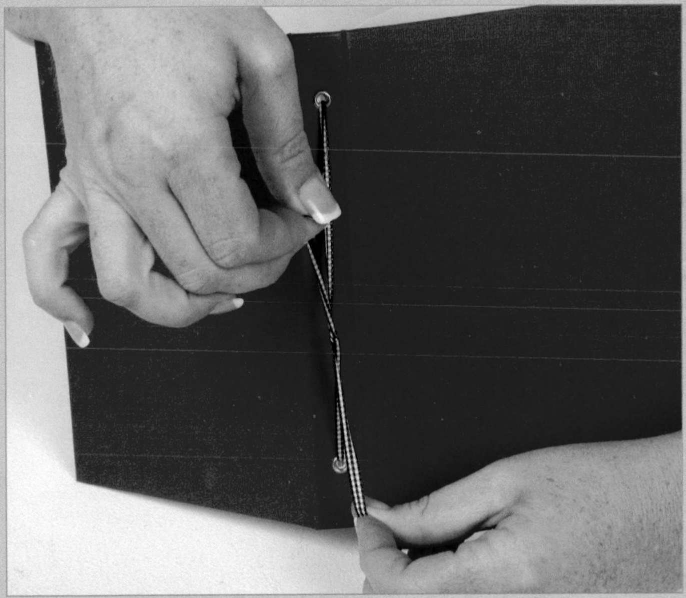

Fast binding is very versatile. Use ribbon, waxed linen thread, fibers, twill tape, pipe cleaners or whatever else your heart desires.

Fast Binding

This simple technique for binding is the perfect way to add signatures to Bazzill Basic Paper's Gated Albums, Cover Alls Albums, and Zippered Albums.

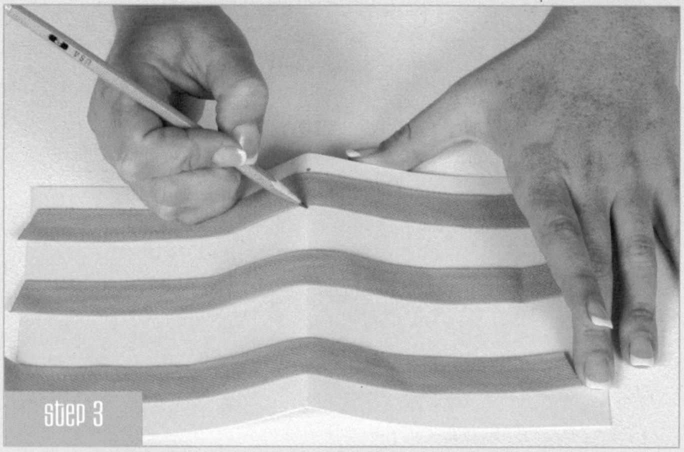

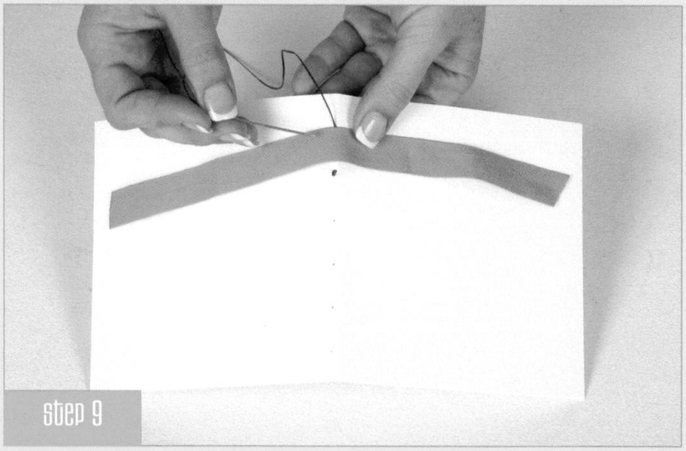

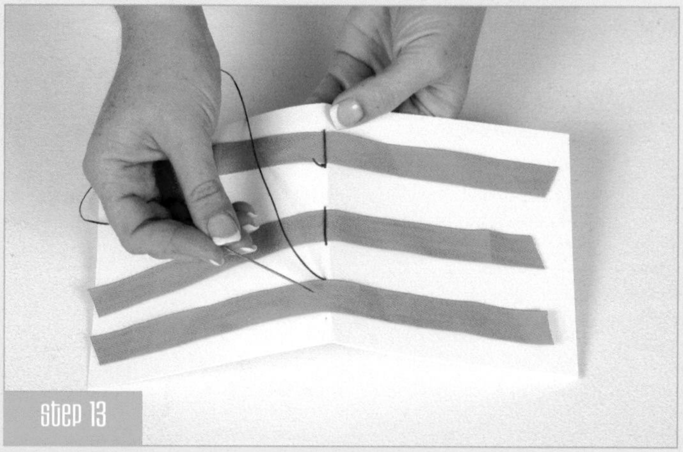

Hop, Skip, & a Jump Binding

Before beginning, cover the outside of the book with additional paper or make sure the twill lines up with the predrilled holes. You don't want the holes in the spine to show.

1. Fold all cardstock in half. Each signature has two pieces of paper.
2. Cut three to five pieces of twill tape depending on the amount of spine you need to cover. Cut each piece 8" (if tying a knot) or 15" (if tying a bow).
3. Set the twill tape in position along the outside spine of one signature and use a pencil to mark in the crease, above and below twill tape.
4. Using a needle or awl, punch through one signature at the pencil marks. Hold the paper like a "V" to make it easier to poke a hole through the crease of the paper. Using the first set of signatures as a template, line up the next signature behind it and punch each hole through the next set. Repeat until all the signatures are punched.
5. Thread a needle with a 54" single strand of waxed linen. Tie a knot.
6. Beginning at the second hole in the spine, insert the needle from the outside, pulling through to the inside. Stop when the knot is firmly against the outside of paper.
7. Insert the needle in the first inside hole and pull through to the outside.
8. Fold twill tape in half to find center and position it across fold between the first and second holes.

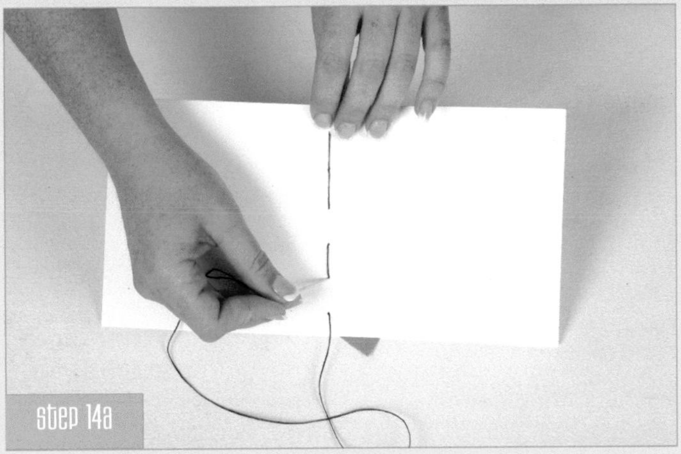

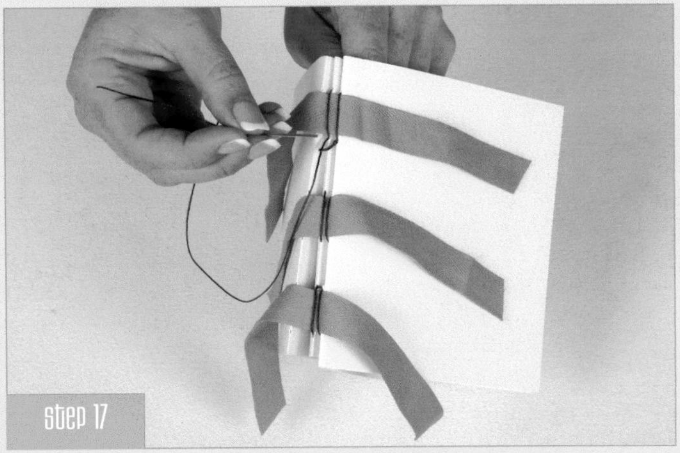

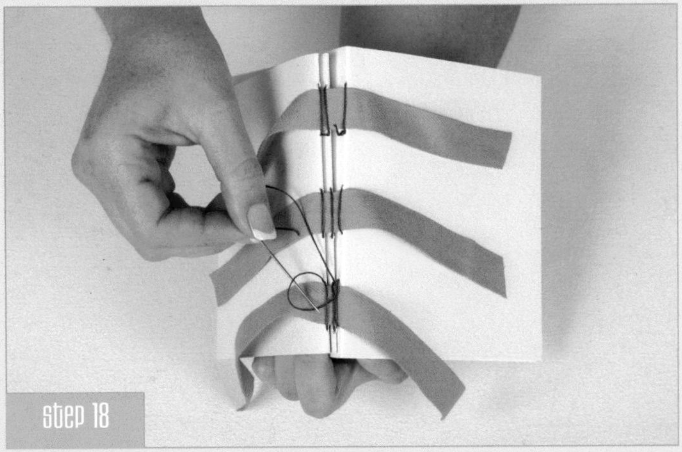

This fun technique is great for adding signatures to so many Bazzill Basic Paper Albums. Try it with the Cover Alls and if you are feeling adventurous try it on the Gated Album. It is a little more difficult, but easily mastered. It will soon be your favorite.

9. Insert needle back into the second hole (thread will cross twill tape) and pull through to inside.
10. Insert needle in third hole and pull through to outside. Use the same technique mentioned above to position twill tape between third and fourth holes.
11. Insert needle in fourth hole (thread will cross twill tape) and pull through to inside.
12. Insert needle in back into the fifth hole and pull through to outside. Add twill tape between fifth and sixth holes.
13. Insert needle in sixth hole (thread will cross twill tape) and pull through to inside.
14. Insert needle in fifth hole and pull through to outside. Align another signature even with the edges of the first one, making sure to position it underneath the twill. Insert needle in the fifth hole and pull through to inside.
15. Insert needle in the sixth hole and pull through to outside. Insert needle in fifth hole (thread will cross twill tape) and pull through to inside.
16. Insert needle in fourth hole and pull through to outside, and so on, and so on.
17. Continue repeating the same steps up the spine of the signature. Alternate adding signatures at the top and bottom of spine.
18. Once all signatures have been added, the final knot will tie on the outside of signature.

(continued on next page)

step 19a

step 19b

step 19c

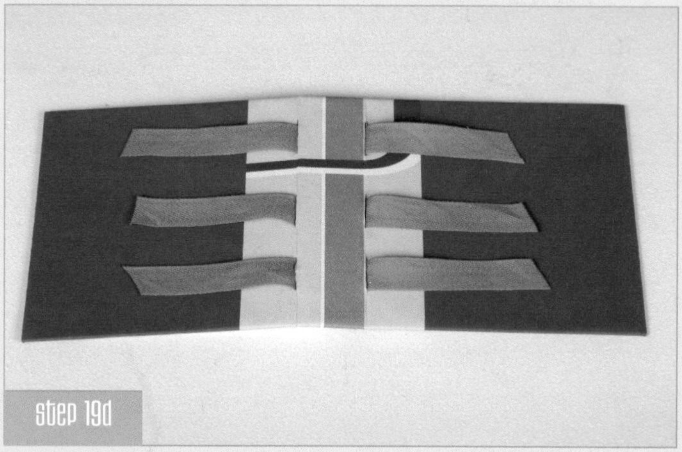

step 19d

step 19e

19. Insert all signatures into album center and mark where the twill lines up on each side of the spine. Using a utility knife, cut a slit that is the same width as the twill tape into each side of the fold of the spine. Slip twill tape from one side of signature through holes. Slip twill tape from other side of signature through holes. Tie twill tape in a knot or bow along outside of spine.

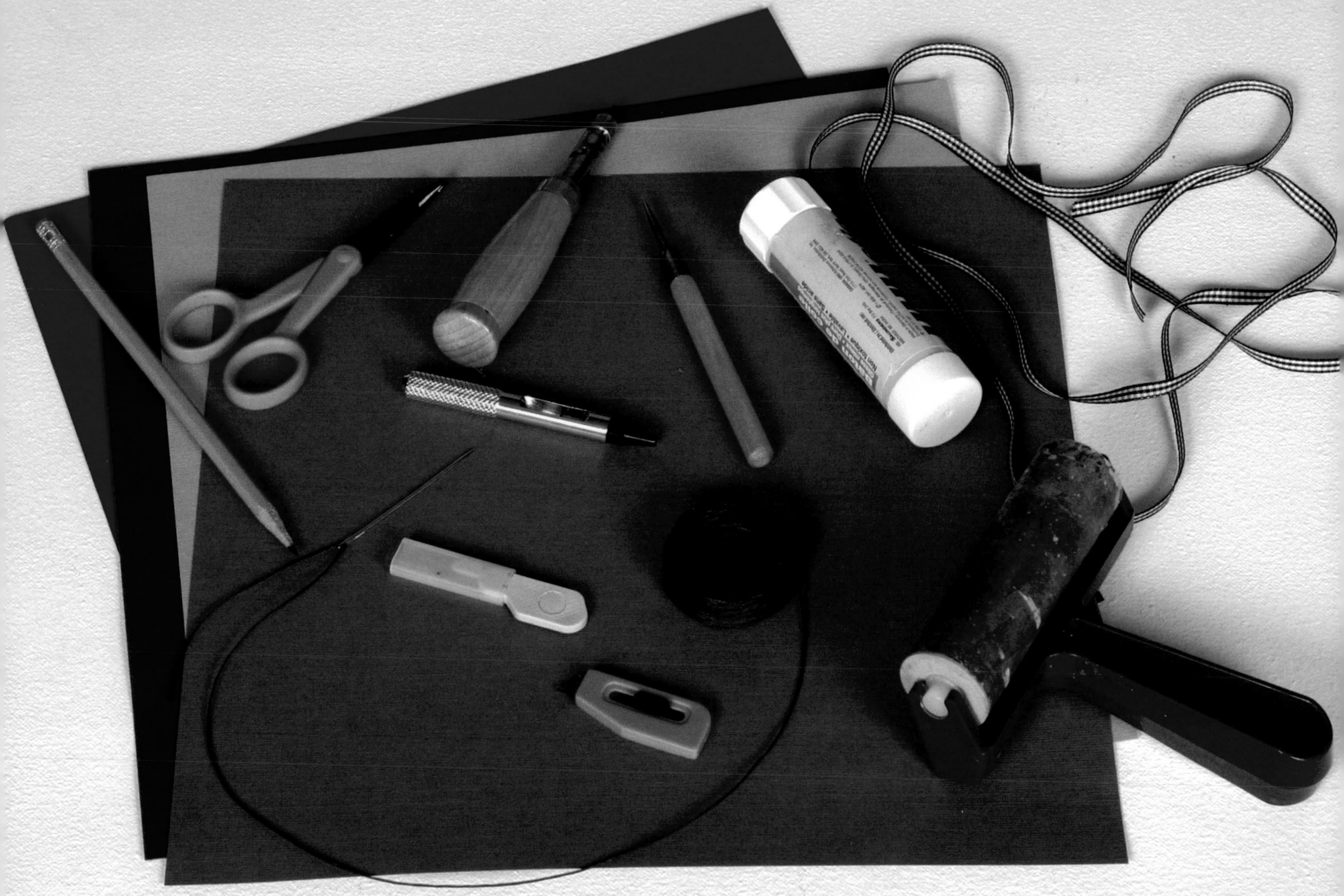

Supply List

- Paper
- Awl or Paper Piercing Tool
- Brayer
- Pencil
- Glue Stick
- Needle
- Waxed Linen Thread
- Eyelet Setter
- Japanese Screw Punch or Anywhere Hole Punch
- Utility Knife

Hot
fun
Fun

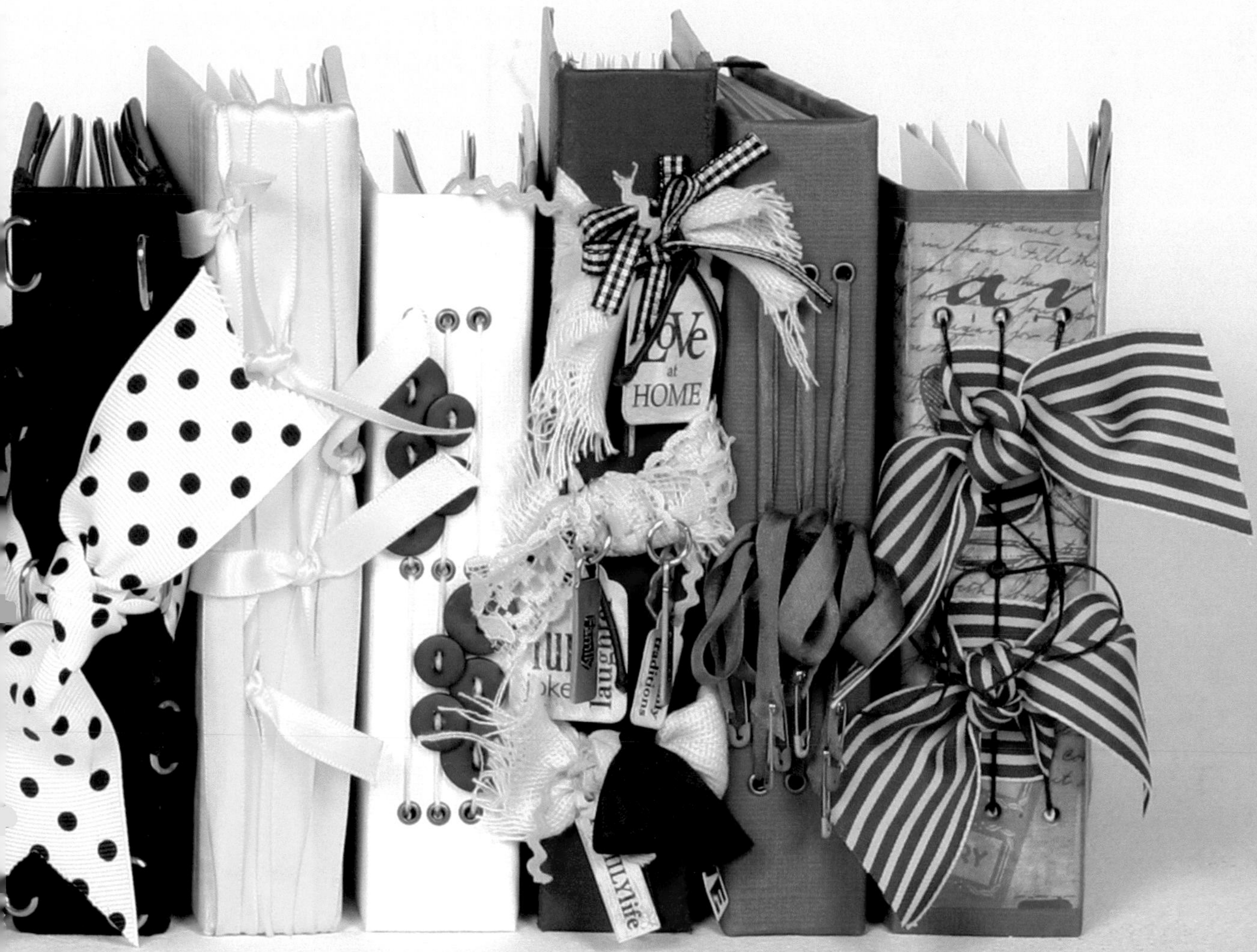

The projects and instructions shown in this book are intended as suggestions and inspirations, and we did our best to provide accurate instructions. However, Bazzill Basics Paper is not liable for any errors, inaccuracies, or omissions.

Designer Q&A

Q. Who has three grandchildren, is a compulsive neat-freak, and makes killer orange rolls?

A. Pam Black

Q. Who has a tattoo, wears a size 11 shoe, and is afraid of alligators and clowns?

A. Amy Totty

Q. Who had her 1st pedicure at 43, met her husband at the grocery store, and hates veggies?

A. Kelli Collins

Q. Who had braces on the day she was married, is pregnant right now, and is a fourth generation native Arizonan?

A. Eva Flake